QUANTUM HYPNOSIS SCRIPTS
Neo-Ericksonian Scripts To Supercharge Your Sessions!

Jo Ana Starr PhD

Second Edition

ISBN-13:
978-1-939427-23-6

TABLE OF CONTENTS

CHAPTER 1

INTRODUCTION

Quantum Hypnosis Scripts is a book of Hypnosis scripts, ideal for either professional use or for Self Hypnosis, and as the title suggests, this book focuses solely on Hypnosis scripts and instructions for their ideal use.

For more comprehensive information on the process of Self Hypnosis, please check out *Quantum Self Hypnosis*, also written by Dr. Starr.

Quantum Hypnosis Scripts includes 24 Hypnosis scripts plus 2 Master Hypnosis Inductions, which are essential to the use of the provided Hypnosis scripts. Included in that total script count are 2 Hypnosis Programs of 3 Hypnosis scripts each, for Weight Loss and Stress Reduction. Since these applications are ideally treated with a series of sessions, they are included here for the reader's use.

By the way, if you are a proponent of Instant Self Hypnosis, reading these complete and simple scripts should work very well for you.

Readers of *Quantum Hypnosis Scripts* receive a FREE full-length Hypnosis audio session, valued at $59, available at the book's website. Detailed information on how to get your free Hypnosis audio session is available in the last chapter of this book.

The Self Hypnosis scripts presented in this book are full-length, professional Hypnosis scripts. By the way, for readers of *Quantum Self Hypnosis* and students or graduates of NEIH, there are no duplicate Hypnosis behavior modification scripts in this book, although the script framework (the beach scene) is used in all the included scripts. There are also a few important, duplicate applications. The general approach for many of the included scripts is ego-strengthening which scripts are generally hard to find, and very helpful for Hypnosis and Hypnotherapy clients as well as Self-Hypnotists. Also important, there are no scripts in this book based on negative programming or aversion therapy. These scripts are all positive, present tense, and affirmative in nature, thus very effective.

This book was written as a companion book to *Quantum Self Hypnosis*, so readers of that book will find many new and interesting scripts to use from this book.

For those unfamiliar with the author, Jo Ana Starr PhD has worked in the field of Hypnotherapy since 1987. She is a Certified Clinical Hypnotherapist and Executive Director of the New England Institute of Hypnotherapy, an award-winning training program operating since 1995. Dr. Starr trained in 1987 with the American Institute of Hypnotherapy under the tutelage of the esteemed Dr. Krasner. She later earned a PhD and holds a Doctorate in Divinity as well. Her undergraduate work was in English, Education, and Psychology. Dr. Starr has made numerous appearances on both radio and television programs to discuss topics such as Hypnosis and Wellness. She is in the process of completing several other books on related topics,

and has authored 8 training programs, all focused on
Hypnosis, Prosperity, Diet and Wellness.

CHAPTER 2

HYPNOSIS SESSION SCRIPTS

As mentioned in the last chapter, the scripts included here are complete Hypnosis Session Scripts. They need only the addition of a Master Hypnosis Induction (included here) on the front end and you're ready to go.

We have included 2 Master Hypnosis Inductions- one full length induction and one a quick induction, so if you don't have a favorite Master Hypnosis Induction, either of the included inductions will work well for you. We have even included the Count-Up script component as part of each Hypnosis session script, as some readers have requested that we do. These are push-button scripts, ready to use instantly.

If you are using a Quick Induction without a count-down component on the front end, you can still use the full

Hypnosis session script with the Count-Up component, if you choose. When a subject is fully hypnotized, a Count-up does help him/her to come back to the present time more easily, so even if you haven't used a Count-down on the front end of the session, it's still perfectly okay to use a Count-up at the end.

By the way, each included script has a minimum of 8 different hypnotic suggestions interwoven into it, with repetitions throughout the script. If you choose to modify these scripts, you can do so by adding additional suggestions which you will repeat throughout the Hypnosis session script.

We have decided to include a Stop Smoking hypnosis script in this book at the 11th hour. This is not a unique script or application, but not including a Stop Smoking script in this Hypnosis script book seemed wrong. I know we promised all new scripts, but this one is not, so consider it a bonus add-on to the original manuscript.

SLEEP WELL HYPNOSIS SCRIPT

As you continue to move along the beach, you feel the sun warming the top of your head, and you feel the sea breeze against your skin, and you hear the sounds of children's laughter. To your right, you see the ocean, and the sun as it dances on the surface of the ocean. You can hear the sounds of sea gulls as they fly above the water, and as they dive into the water, happy to be alive, just like you, and as you continue to breathe deeply filling your lungs with life-giving oxygen, the colors of the children's swimsuits catch your eye... bright reds, and lemon yellows, and sky blues. You are amazed at the remarkable beauty of this place, and you feel great... happy, healthy, glad to be alive... glad to be here, and glad to be you. At bedtime, you fall easily and deeply into sleep. As soon as your head hits the pillow, you nod off easily and effortlessly.

As you continue to walk along the beach, you enjoy feeling healthy and whole; you realize that this magical place has

caused a complete transformation in you. You realize that you have left behind the concern that brought you here today. Sleep is your friend and you love to sleep. When you go to bed, you fall asleep immediately. You feel free, and healthy, and strong, as you move along the beach. You breathe deeply, filling your lungs with life-giving oxygen, and as you move along the beach, you notice that your clothes are a little loose, and you feel that you are releasing a little excess weight in the process of leaving this challenge behind you. At bedtime, the cares of the day evaporate and you sleep effortlessly

As you continue to move along the beach, you notice a large group of people ahead on your right. These people are active, and happy, playing with a beach ball while others are playing volleyball. You breathe deeply as you walk along, and as you do, you feel your youth returning, and your breath deepening, and you feel grateful to be here, and happy to be you. You marvel at your body's ability to easily and effortlessly leave behind the challenge that brought you here today. Your mind rests when your body rests. You love to go to bed because you sleep so easily and peacefully.

As you continue along the beach, you breathe deeply and easily. You feel your clothes growing looser on your body, as your metabolism adjusts favorably to the changes you are making. You feel your body strengthen, and as it does, your metabolism improves, in fact, your entire body responds favorably to these changes. Sleep is a friend at your side from the moment you decide to sleep.

You realize that it is time to head back the way you came, and you turn around on the beach, heading back toward the path. You wave at your new friends, still playing and laughing and expressing all the health and well-being they enjoy, and you feel grateful to be a part of that group of healthy and happy people. You love to sleep. You fall asleep easily and effortlessly.

You realize you are completely free of the challenge that brought you here today, and that you no longer have the concerns that brought you here today. You realize you have been given a second chance at complete health and happiness, and you are grateful to your mind and body for the opportunity. Your mind rests when your body rests.

As you continue to move along the path, you feel strong and free, healthy and happy, glad to be here, and glad to be you. As you continue along the path, you hear the seagulls, and the ocean waves, and you feel the sun warming your head and your shoulders, you feel the breeze against your skin, as you breathe deeply and freely, filling your lungs with life-giving oxygen. And as you continue to move along the path, you realize that we are coming closer to the pastoral area with the barn, and you look back one more time to see this beautiful place, and to remember evermore, how wonderful and alive you feel now that you are free of the challenge that brought you here today. You breathe deeply and easily when you go to bed.

As you continue to move along the path, your feet touch the gravel and as you look around, you notice the duck pond up ahead on the left and the red barn up ahead on the right. The cows are still grazing peacefully and the leaves rustle in the breeze. You see the large oak door up ahead and move forward toward it.

You arrive at the door and pull it open, the hinges squeaking again. You are now in the large round foyer with the stairs up ahead. You move toward the stairs and start up them.

Number 1

Number 2

Number 3.......Coming back.

Number 4.......Coming back.

Number 5.......Coming back slowly.......coming back.

Number 6.......Coming back to the current moment and place.....coming back.

Number 7.......Coming back...feeling rested and refreshed....coming back.

Number 8.......Coming back...feeling good, feeling fine, perfectly relaxed.

Number 9...... Coming back now, eyes open, wide awake, eyes open, wide awake.

Number 10.....Eyes open, wide awake, eyes open wide awake.

REMEMBER EASILY HYPNOSIS SCRIPT

As you continue to move along the beach, you feel the sun warming the top of your head, and you feel the sea breeze against your skin, and you hear the sounds of children's laughter. To your right, you see the ocean, and the sun as it dances on the surface of the ocean. You can hear the sounds of sea gulls as they fly above the water, and as they dive into the water, happy to be alive, just like you, and as you continue to breathe deeply filling your lungs with life-giving oxygen, the colors of the children's swimsuits catch your eye...bright reds, and lemon yellows, and sky blues.

You are amazed at the remarkable beauty of this place, and you feel great... happy, healthy, glad to be alive... glad to be here, and glad to be you. Happily, you have the memory of an elephant; you never forget anything.

As you continue to walk along the beach, you enjoy feeling healthy and whole; you realize that this magical place has

caused a complete transformation for you. You realize that you have left behind the habit that brought you here today. When you read to learn something new, you retain all the information you have read. You feel free, and healthy, and strong, as you move along the beach. You breathe deeply, filling your lungs with life-giving oxygen, and as you move along the beach, you notice that your clothes are a little loose, and you feel that you may be releasing an extra 3-5 pounds in the process of leaving this habit behind you. You are smart and you remember everything you choose to remember. You can even remember events from childhood when you choose to.

As you continue to move along the beach, you notice a large group of people ahead on your right. These people are active and happy, playing with a beach ball while others are playing volleyball. These people are active, trim, and happy people. You breathe deeply as you walk along, and as you do, you feel your youth returning, and your breath deepening, and you feel grateful to be here, and happy to be you. You marvel at your body's ability to easily and effortlessly leave behind the challenge that brought you here today. You can easily remember birthdays, anniversaries, sport scores, and more.

As you continue along the beach, you breathe deeply and easily. You feel your clothes growing loose on your body, as your metabolism adjusts favorably to the changes you are making. You feel your body strengthen, and as it does, your metabolism improves, in fact, your entire body responds favorably to these changes. Your mind is limitless, so you can remember everything you want to remember.

You realize that it is time to turn back the way you came, and you turn around on the beach, heading back toward the path. You wave at your new friends, still playing and laughing and expressing all the health and well-being they enjoy, and you feel grateful to be part of that group of healthy and happy people. You can remember in infinite detail all the happy memories you have stored away in your mind.

You realize you are completely free of the challenge that brought you here today. You realize you have been given a second chance at complete health and happiness, and you are grateful to your body for the opportunity. Your past is past in name only. Your can access the information about all past events as if they happened yesterday.

As you continue to move along the path, you feel strong and free, healthy and happy, glad to be here, and glad to be you. As you continue along the path, you hear the seagulls, and the ocean waves, and you feel the sun warming your head and your shoulders, you feel the breeze against your skin, as you breathe deeply and freely, filling your lungs with life-giving oxygen. You are blessed with a remarkable memory; everyone says so. And as you continue to move along the path, you realize that we are coming closer to the pastoral area with the barn, and you look back one more time to see this beautiful place, and to remember evermore, how wonderful and alive you feel now that you are free of the challenge that brought you here today. You remember everything easily and effortlessly.

As you continue to move along the path, your feet touch the gravel and as you look around, you notice the duck pond up ahead on the left and the red barn up ahead on the right. The cows are still grazing peacefully and the leaves rustle in the breeze. You see the large oak door up ahead and move forward toward it.

You arrive at the door and pull it open, the hinges squeaking again. You are now in the large round foyer with the stairs up ahead. You move toward the stairs and start up them.

Number 1

Number 2

Number 3.......Coming back.

Number 4.......Coming back.

Number 5.......Coming back slowly.......coming back.

Number 6.......Coming back to the current moment and place.....coming back.

Number 7.......Coming back...feeling rested and refreshed....coming back.

Number 8.......Coming back...feeling good, feeling fine, perfectly relaxed.

Number 9...... Coming back now, eyes open, wide awake, eyes open, wide awake.

Number 10.....Eyes open, wide awake, eyes open wide awake.

FINDING YOUR TRUE LOVE HYPNOSIS SCRIPT

As you continue to move along the beach, you feel the sun warming the top of your head, and you feel the sea breeze against your skin, and you hear the sounds of children's laughter. To your right, you see the ocean, and the sun as it dances on the surface of the ocean. You can hear the sounds of sea gulls as they fly above the water, and as they dive into the water, happy to be alive, just like you, and as you continue to breathe deeply filling your lungs with life-giving oxygen, the colors of the children's swimsuits catch your eye... bright reds, and lemon yellows, and sky blues. You are amazed at the remarkable beauty of this place, and you feel great... happy, healthy, glad to be alive... glad to be here, and glad to be you. You are love, loved and lovable.

As you continue to walk along the beach, you enjoy feeling healthy and whole; you realize that this magical place has caused a complete transformation for you. You realize that you have left behind the challenge that brought you here today. You feel lovable and ready to find your true love. You feel free, and healthy, and strong, as you move along the beach. You breathe deeply, filling your lungs with life-giving oxygen, and as you move along the beach, you notice that your clothes are a little loose, and you feel that you are releasing a few extra pounds which is always good. You are surrounded by love. You cannot remember where you end and the love begins; you and love are so completely entwined.

As you continue to move along the beach, you notice a large group of people ahead on your right. These people are active, and happy, playing with a beach ball while others are playing volleyball. These people are active, trim, and happy, and as you observe these people, you feel a sense of love of them...their innocent happiness. You breathe deeply as you walk along, and as you do, you feel your youth returning, and your breath deepening, and you feel grateful to be here, and happy to be you. You marvel at your body's ability to easily and effortlessly help you to achieve the goal that brought you here today. Finding your true love is easy; you invite your Beloved to join you now.

As you continue along the beach, you breathe deeply and easily. You feel your clothes growing loose on your body, as your metabolism adjusts favorably to the changes you are making. You feel your body strengthen, and as it does, your metabolism improves, in fact, your entire body responds favorably to these changes. You know that you will recognize your true love when you see him/her.

You realize that it is time to return back the way you came, and you turn around on the beach, heading back toward the path, and you wave at your new friends, still playing and laughing and expressing all the health and well-being they enjoy, and you feel grateful to be a part of that group of healthy, happy and loving people. You welcome deep and abiding love into your life. You deeply desire the happiness that true love can provide, and you welcome it in.

You realize you are in the process of achieving the ideal outcome that brought you here today. You realize you have been given a second chance at love and happiness, and you are grateful to your mind and body for the opportunity. You love to see older couples holding hands; they are a symbol to you of lasting love and as you continue to walk along the beach, you notice several older couples talking and laughing with each other. This sight always makes you smile.

As you continue to move along the path, you feel strong and free, healthy and happy, glad to be here, and glad to be you. As you continue along the path, you hear the seagulls, and the ocean waves, and you feel the sun warming your head and your shoulders, you feel the breeze against your skin, as you breathe deeply and freely, filling your lungs with life-giving oxygen. You believe in lasting love and invite it into your life. And as you continue to move along the path, you realize that we are coming closer to the pastoral area with the barn, and you look back one more time to see this beautiful place, and to remember evermore, how wonderful and alive you feel now that you are free of the challenge that brought you here today. You are free to love deeply and you choose to do so now.

As you continue to move along the path, your feet touch the gravel and as you look around, you notice the duck pond up ahead on the left and the red barn up ahead on the right side of the path. The cows are still grazing peacefully and the leaves rustle in the breeze. You see the large oak door up ahead and move forward toward it.

You arrive at the door and pull it open, the hinges squeaking again. You are now in the large round foyer with the stairs up ahead. You move toward the stairs and start to move up them.

Number 1

Number 2

Number 3.......Coming back.

Number 4.......Coming back.

Number 5.......Coming back slowly.......coming back.

Number 6.......Coming back to the current moment and place.....coming back.

Number 7.......Coming back...feeling rested and refreshed....coming back.

Number 8.......Coming back...feeling good, feeling fine, perfectly relaxed.

Number 9...... Coming back now, eyes open, wide awake, eyes open, wide awake.

Number 10.....Eyes open, wide awake, eyes open wide awake.

I HAVE LIVED BEFORE HYPNOSIS SCRIPT

This is a classic Past Life Regression hypnosis script and the only one I've ever used. I think you'll like it.

[Please use one of the Master Hypnosis Inductions to induce the appropriate medium state of Hypnosis and then proceed with the following script.]

[Script begins]

I'm going to count down from 10 to 1. Allow yourself to relax fully and completely. Don't concern yourself with the process, just trust that you will receive the benefits you desire.

[Slowly 10, 9, 8, 7, 6, 5, 4, 3, 2 and 1.] And now you can just close your eyes, and you can keep them closed. It was just to relax your eyelids. And right now, in your eyelids there is probably a feeling of relaxation...and you find this a pleasant sensation.

[If the client or yourself does not seem to be at the proper stage of relaxation- fidgety, or rapid respiration, or nervous eyelid blinking, go thru the 10-1 count-down again slowly, or you may vary it to going down a spiraling staircase as you count down the numbers.]

I will count rapidly now---   10, 9, 8, 7, 6, 5, 4, 3, 2 and 1. You are now at your own natural level of relaxation. And from this level you may move to any of level with complete awareness, and you can function at will. You are completely in control at every level of mind, and you can accept or reject anything that is given here to you today.

You are in control. There is something you long to discover, and so our journey begins.

My voice is your guide, and as we progress, you discover that you can listen to my voice, and also deal with other things at the same time. You are a person of many abilities, so my voice does not distract you as we continue along our journey. You can relax...you don't need to try to do anything...your subconscious is here and can hear every word that I am saying.

As you take a deep breath, you feel yourself drifting; you feel less and less need to listen closely to my voice. In your own time, today, tomorrow, next week, your subconscious mind will reveal what it has uncovered to you in a dream, or at a moment of consciousness, but at the perfect moment in the perfect way. You will be given memories of other times and places, memories you thought were gone, only to be discovered again. And with these newly found memories comes new insights, new growth, new understanding. And stored deep in your subconscious mind are wonderful memories. Your subconscious mind can access and recall these memories and bring them back with you later.

So, by looking deeply into your mind, you can see your soul's vision and hear the voices of experiences captured far in the past. Your subconscious mind can access these memories and bring them back to you later.

Can you remember a time in your life when you really felt safe?

[Pause]

And you may begin going back to around the time you were 18 years old - choosing a pleasant and happy memory of about the time you were 18 years old. You will find that this is very easy for you to do - choosing one specific memory or event - and just simply focusing on it, looking at the people around you and then looking at yourself.

I will be quiet and give you plenty of time to simply enjoy this event. You may hear voices or you may simply feel the presence of people. You may see as clearly as in a movie, or the images may be vague. You may see these things in your mind's eye, you may hear voices and sounds from this time whispered in your ear. You may only sense the memory. It doesn't matter. It doesn't really matter in what way you perceive your memories. You are about 18 years old now. What is happening?

[LONG PAUSE]

Now you may continue going back to about the time you were 5 or 6 years old. Again choosing a pleasant happy memory, an impression, or a specific experience from about the time you were 6 years old. Focus on this experience; look at this memory clearly. See what you were wearing, sense or feel the people around you. Look and listen to the information. Allow yourself to watch these experiences as if you were sitting in the seats of a movie theater. You are not re-experiencing this; you are just observing the 6 year old you. You are 6 years old now.

[LONG PAUSE]

Now continue going back to about the time you were 4, and then 3, and then 2, and now 1. And keep going back to the time of your birth. And going even beyond that to that warm and safe place from which we all come. You are where nothing can harm you; you are perfectly safe, perfectly secure, perfectly protected, perfectly at peace. You feel loved and completely warm and protected. This is the time of your beginning, of growing, a time of movement, and a time of preparation. This is a very good time, and you can travel beyond this time and place as well.

You are now going into the Rose Mist that feels so soft and safe. And the Rose Mist surrounds you and protects you. You are very safe and comfortable here; the Rose Mist is a time of inner peace, tranquility, quiet movement, gentle sounds, and gentle light. You like it here very much because you can experience real peace and serenity, real joy here. You are so comfortable here, and yet a part of you longs for more - movement, life; and this longing grows within you until it becomes stronger and stronger. And this desire allows you to look outward, and as you look outward, you see a light, as if you were looking down a long tunnel. The light is good. You feel drawn toward the light and you feel yourself moving toward the light. You are traveling along the pathway of the soul. The light enters you thru the top of your head and fills you with light. The light heals you... protects you... surrounds you... as you feel life energy flowing thru your being; you feel a quickening in you which is life. You realize that you now exist in separation from the Mist and other beings and that you are in incarnate form. This realization comes over you and you want to understand it. You allow yourself to look down towards your feet and you notice what you are wearing on your feet. Plant your feet and your consciousness firmly on the ground and notice what you are wearing on your feet. Don't allow yourself to analyze the experience, but just glance down and mentally record what you are wearing on your feet, and what you sense or feel about this moment. You may wish to say this aloud. What are you wearing on your feet?

[PAUSE]

And now you can continue looking up your body, at what you may have on the bottom half of your body. Feel the texture... determine whether it is fabric or metal or animal skin... see the colors of your garment. Continue looking up the body now, and look at what you have on the top half of your body. Now allow yourself to glimpse the entire body and I will be quiet for a moment. What are you wearing?

What is covering all or part of your body? What sort of body do you have?

[PAUSE]

Notice any jewelry you may be wearing, and allow yourself to observe whether you are wearing anything on your head and whether you have any jewelry on your hands. Focus on allowing yourself to take in as much information as possible. Allow yourself to see clearly as you peacefully and gently explore the scene around you. Process this information and if possible, take a mental picture of it. Look at your entire body, and I will be quiet for a moment. Are you wearing jewelry? Are you wearing adornments of any sort?

[PAUSE]

Now, with your mind's eye, look around slowly to see where you are situated and make a note of it. Are there trees, mountains, sand, the ocean, a lake, a stream, or buildings? Look around and record what you see. And again I will be quiet while you make a full turn around yourself, looking in all directions, and making a note of the important things you see. Mentally record as much of this information as you can so that you can examine it later. What do you see? Is it a familiar scene or is it some place entirely new to you?

[PAUSE]

And now, you may look for other people. Who is around you... how are they dressed... are you in a group of men, or women, or are you alone? If you are alone, you may look to another time when there are people around you. Make a note of these people, and record the information mentally so you may access it at a later time. If there are people, do they look familiar? Is there someone special nearby... someone with whom you have a special relationship or a special fondness? Look around you... perhaps there is a child or an adult who is dear to you. Are you part of a community or are you one of only a few other people present? Mentally record these feelings and impressions.

If you listen closely, you may even hear names being mentioned. Who is there with you?

[PAUSE]

And now you may look for a vehicle of transportation... something you may have ridden on or in. Are there carriages, or wagons, or beasts of burden? Is there someone there who is currently using a means of transportation? Make a note of the means of transportation. Do you see any forms of conveyance? Is this a place of commerce, activity and many forms of conveyance or it is a quiet, less active place? Answer these questions either out loud or in your mind so that you can review this information later.

[PAUSE]

And at this time, you may feel hungry. What is it that you eat when you are hungry? Can you smell the food cooking? Are you able to taste it? Are there smells of food or cooking? Is there a store or place to buy food items near you? If so, what does it look like? Record your impressions. What do you see and smell?

[PAUSE]

And now, if your listen quietly, you may hear friends call out your name to you. What is it? What are you doing... what is your work or your job. Do you seem to have an occupation or something that occupies your time? If you don't work, are you a student? If so, what are you learning?

[PAUSE]

And as you look around yourself for clues, do you get an impression of where you are? What land is this? What is this land called... what is the name of this place? Are you in a forest, a desert, a mountain top or valley? Or are you in a city with public transportation, lots of people and lots of activity? Perhaps you can sense what century or what year this is. Do you know what year this is? Ask someone who is close to you or look for a newspaper or printed calendar?

[PAUSE]

And now you may move to a major event in your life, a time that has important meaning for you, and focus on what is happening. This may be a big event or a small event; it doesn't matter as long as it has significance for you. Can you recollect or return to the moment of a major event in your life?

[PAUSE]

And what is happening next? What moments follow the event of importance to you?

[PAUSE]

And what is happening now... what are you doing?

[PAUSE]

And now in a detached way, as a bystander, look at the time of your death in this incarnation. Death is simply the next stage of life. What events have led up to your death? How did you die? Allow yourself to witness these events without feeling them in a painful way. What do you experience after your death? Look at the death experience and ask to assimilate its messages.

[PAUSE]

What is the reason or purpose for this life? What are the lessons for your Soul? Was it a happy life? What made you the happiest in this life? Was anything left uncompleted in this life? If so, you may return to complete it. Take your time; I will wait for you.

[LONG PAUSE]

And now that you have received all this information, bring it all together into a vivid symbol or a series of symbols, and wrap it up in something familiar to you, so that you can bring all this information back with you. Encode this information in your mind in a way that will make it easy to access. Allow yourself to encapsulate this experience and trust that you will be able to access the information that has value for your present life and that you will release the information that has no value for your present life.

Most important of all, mentally look into your own eyes and the eyes of those around you, and those you have loved, and that special person. Look into the eyes of everyone you saw and send love from your eyes to their eyes. And as you bless them, forgive them, and send them your love, they begin to fade. And as they begin to fade, let them go. Release them, bless them, forgive them, and let them go as they bless and forgive you. Let the veil drop slowly. Allow the curtain to slowly close, and allow a full healing of this life and of this time.

[PAUSE]

And as you slowly begin coming back, traveling thru time and space, you can bring back with you all that was positive, interesting, and significant to you. Simply release and close the door on information or impressions that are not necessary for your soul growth at this time. Bring back only that which has value for you. You will retain in you conscious mind only what is helpful and beneficial to you at this time.

Now you are coming back to and thru the light, once again traveling on the avenue of the soul, where all things are known to you thru that warm and safe place where nothing can harm your returning thru the levels of the mind to the clear recall of your own mind, and bringing back the information that you have recorded. Slowly now, slowly now, coming back to the present life to _____ (date) in _____ (city, state). Plant your feet firmly in the present... step fully and happily into your present life.

And in a little while, when you are fully awake, you will feel just wonderful. You will feel better than before. You will be wide awake, clear-headed, and happy and you will feel relaxed, refreshed, happy to be alive and happy to be you. Your subconscious mind always protects you and knows what is best for you.

[Slowly count back up. Take your time.]

I will count from 1 to 10. At the count of 10, you can open your eyes, be wide awake, feeling great, feeling fine, happy to be alive and happy to be awake. I will count now.

#1 - coming back very slowly now; #2 - coming back very slowly now; #3 - coming up now; #4 - feel your energy returning to you; #5 - feeling totally normal and perfectly fine; #6 - feeling re-energized; #7 - coming up to your full potential; #8 - fully awake and fully aware of your surroundings; #9 - feeling revitalized; #10 - wide-awake-open your eyes now-wide-awake.

[After you are out of your session, take notes about this past life regression. Number and date the session notes in case you decide to do other past life regressions.]

JOYFUL EXERCISE HYPNOSIS SCRIPT

As you continue to move along the beach, you feel the sun warming the top of your head, and you feel the sea breeze against your skin, and you hear the sounds of children's laughter. To your right, you see the ocean, and the sun as it dances on the surface of the ocean. You can hear the sounds of sea gulls as they fly above the water, and as they dive into the water, happy to be alive, just like you, and as you continue to breathe deeply filling your lungs with life-giving oxygen, the colors of the children's swimsuits catch your eye... bright reds, and lemon yellows, and sky blues. You are amazed at the remarkable beauty of this place, and you feel great... happy, healthy, glad to be alive... glad to be here, and glad to be you. You love doing things that feel good and exercise feels good.

As you continue to walk along the beach, you enjoy feeling healthy and whole; you realize that this magical place has caused a complete transformation for you. You realize that

you have left behind the cares that brought you here today. You love to feel your muscles working hard-it makes you feel happy. You feel free, and healthy, and strong, as you move along the beach. You breathe deeply, filling your lungs with life-giving oxygen, and as you move along the beach, you notice that your clothes are a little looser, and you feel that you are releasing a few extra pounds in the process of leaving this challenge behind you. You love to breathe deeply as you exercise. It's so easy for you to breathe deeply and freely.

As you continue to move along the beach, you notice a large group of people ahead on your right. These people are active, and happy, playing with a beach ball while others are playing volleyball. These people are active, trim, and happy. You breathe deeply as you walk along, and as you do, you feel your youth returning, and your breath deepening, and you feel grateful to be here, and happy to be you. You marvel at your body's ability to easily and effortlessly deal with the challenge that brought you here today. Your body loves exercise and you love your body, so you exercise joyfully and enthusiastically whenever you can.

As you continue along the beach, you breathe deeply and easily. You feel your clothes growing loose on your body, as your metabolism adjusts favorably to the changes you are making. You feel your body strengthen, and as it does, your metabolism improves, in fact, your entire body responds favorably to these changes. You are happiest when you are moving your body.

You realize that it is time to return back the way you came, and you turn around on the beach, heading back toward the path, and you wave at your new friends, still playing and laughing and expressing all the health and well-being they enjoy, and you feel grateful to be a part of that group of healthy and happy people. Your body responds powerfully to all forms of exercise, which makes you happy.

You realize you are completely aligned with the purpose that brought you here today. You realize you have been given a second chance at complete health and happiness, and you are grateful to your mind and body for the opportunity. You love the feeling of your body moving through space; physical activity is your friend. You love to stretch your body and use your muscles.

As you continue to move along the path, you feel strong and free, healthy and happy, glad to be here, and glad to be you. As you continue along the path, you hear the seagulls, and the ocean waves, and you feel the sun warming your head and your shoulders, you feel the breeze against your skin, as you breathe deeply and freely, filling your lungs with life-giving oxygen. You love your body and your body loves exercise, so you exercise as often as you can. And as you continue to move along the path, you realize that we are coming closer to the pastoral area with the barn, and you look back one more time to see this beautiful place, and to remember evermore, how wonderful and alive you feel now that you are free of the challenge that brought you here today. You love doing things that feel good and exercise feels good.

As you continue to move along the path, your feet touch the gravel and as you look around, you notice the duck pond up ahead on the left and the red barn up ahead on the right. The cows are still grazing peacefully and the leaves rustle in the breeze. You see the large oak door up ahead and move forward toward it.

You arrive at the door and pull it open, the hinges squeaking again. You are now in the large round foyer with the stairs up ahead. You move toward the stairs and start up them.

Number 1

Number 2

Number 3.......Coming back.

Number 4.......Coming back.

Number 5.......Coming back slowly.......coming back.

Number 6.......Coming back to the current moment and place.....coming back.

Number 7.......Coming back...feeling rested and refreshed....coming back.

Number 8.......Coming back...feeling good, feeling fine, perfectly relaxed.

Number 9...... Coming back now, eyes open, wide awake, eyes open, wide awake.

Number 10.....Eyes open, wide awake, eyes open wide awake.

I LOVE TAKING TESTS HYPNOSIS SCRIPT

As you continue to move along the beach, you feel the sun warming the top of your head, and you feel the sea breeze against your skin, and you hear the sounds of children's laughter. To your right, you see the ocean, and the sun as it dances on the surface of the ocean. You can hear the sounds of sea gulls as they fly above the water, and as they dive into the water, happy to be alive, just like you, and as you continue to breathe deeply filling your lungs with life-giving oxygen, the colors of the children's swimsuits catch your eye... bright reds, and lemon yellows, and sky blues. You are amazed at the remarkable beauty of this place, and you feel great... happy, healthy, glad to be alive... glad to be here, and glad to be you. Tests are fun for you; they are like games and you love games.

As you continue to walk along the beach, you enjoy feeling healthy and whole; you realize that this magical place has caused a complete transformation for you. You realize that

you have free from the challenge that brought you here today. You enjoy using your mind and test-taking uses your mind in a really productive way. You feel free, and healthy, and strong, as you move along the beach. You breathe deeply, filling your lungs with life-giving oxygen, and as you move along the beach, you notice that your clothes are a little loose, and you feel that you are releasing an extra few pounds in the process of leaving this challenge behind you. You always do well on tests. You expect to do well and you are never disappointed.

As you continue to move along the beach, you notice a large group of people ahead on your right. These people are active, and happy, playing with a beach ball while others are playing volleyball. These people are active, trim, and happy. You breathe deeply as you walk along, and as you do, you feel your youth returning, and your breath deepening, and you feel grateful to be here, and happy to be you. You marvel at your body's ability to easily and effortlessly leave behind the habit that brought you here today. You are a smart person and you love to share your knowledge with others, so sharing what you know on a test is a natural activity for you.

As you continue along the beach, you breathe deeply and easily. You feel your clothes growing looser on your body, as your metabolism adjusts favorably to the changes you are making. You feel your body strengthen, and as it does, your metabolism improves, in fact, your entire body responds favorably to these changes. Tests exercise your mind. Tests are fun to take.

You realize that it is time to return back the way you came, and you turn around on the beach, heading back toward the path, and you wave at your new friends, still playing and laughing and expressing all the health and well-being they enjoy, and you feel grateful to be a part of that group of healthy and happy people. You love knowing that you can ace any test that you are given.

You realize you are completely free of the challenge that brought you here today. You realize you have been given a second chance at complete health and happiness, and you are grateful to your body for the opportunity. Tests are fun-you really enjoy taking tests.

As you continue to move along the path, you feel strong and free, healthy and happy, glad to be here, and glad to be you. As you continue along the path, you hear the seagulls, and the ocean waves, and you feel the sun warming your head and your shoulders, you feel the breeze against your skin, as you breathe deeply and freely, filling your lungs with life-giving oxygen. You look forward to taking tests. As you continue to move along the path, you realize that we are coming closer to the pastoral area with the barn, and you look back one more time to see this beautiful place, and to remember evermore, how wonderful and alive you feel now that you are free of the challenge that brought you here today. You are a smart person who loves to take tests. You love the intellectual challenge that tests represent to you. You love a good challenge.

As you continue to move along the path, your feet touch the gravel and as you look around, you notice the duck pond up ahead on the left and the red barn up ahead on the right. The cows are still grazing peacefully and the leaves rustle in the breeze. You see the large oak door up ahead and move forward toward it.

You arrive at the door and pull it open, the hinges squeaking again. You are now in the large round foyer with the stairs up ahead. You move toward the stairs and start up them.

Number 1

Number 2

Number 3.......Coming back.

Number 4.......Coming back.

Number 5.......Coming back slowly.......coming back.

Number 6.......Coming back to the current moment and place.....coming back.

Number 7.......Coming back...feeling rested and refreshed....coming back.

Number 8.......Coming back...feeling good, feeling fine, perfectly relaxed.

Number 9...... Coming back now, eyes open, wide awake, eyes open, wide awake.

Number 10.....Eyes open, wide awake, eyes open wide awake.

I LOVE ANIMALS HYPNOSIS SCRIPT

As you continue to move along the beach, you feel the sun warming the top of your head, and you feel the sea breeze against your skin, and you hear the sounds of children's laughter. To your right, you see the ocean, and the sun as it dances on the surface of the ocean. You can hear the sounds of sea gulls as they fly above the water, and as they dive into the water, happy to be alive, just like you, and as you continue to breathe deeply filling your lungs with life-giving oxygen, the colors of the children's swimsuits catch your eye... bright reds, and lemon yellows, and sky blues. You are amazed at the remarkable beauty of this place, and you feel great... happy, healthy, glad to be alive... glad to be here, and glad to be you. You love all animals and all animals love you.

As you continue to walk along the beach, you enjoy feeling healthy and whole; you realize that this magical place has caused a complete transformation for you. You realize that

you have left behind the challenge that brought you here today. You love to touch animals; they feel soft and warm. You feel free, and healthy, and strong, as you move along the beach. You breathe deeply, filling your lungs with life-giving oxygen, and as you move along the beach, you notice that your clothes are a little loose, and you feel that you are releasing an extra few pounds in the process of leaving this challenge behind you. You are always happy being around animals.

As you continue to move along the beach, you notice a large group of people ahead on your right. These people are active, and happy, playing with a beach ball while others are playing volleyball. You breathe deeply as you walk along, and as you do, you feel your youth returning, and your breath deepening, and you feel grateful to be here, and happy to be you. You marvel at your body's ability to easily and effortlessly leave behind the challenge that brought you here today. Animals are your friends. You love animals.

As you continue along the beach, you breathe deeply and easily. You feel your clothes growing looser on your body, as your metabolism adjusts favorably to the changes you are making. You feel your body strengthen, and as it does, your metabolism improves, in fact, your entire body responds favorably to these changes. Animals always love you no matter what kind of mood you're in. Animals are happy to listen to all your news.

You realize that it is time to return back the way you came, and you turn around on the beach, heading back toward the path. You wave to your new friends, still playing and laughing and expressing all the health and well-being they enjoy. You feel grateful to be a part of that group of healthy and happy people. You always feel happy when you are talking to or petting an animal.

You realize you are completely free of the challenge that brought you here today. You realize you have been given a second chance at complete health and happiness, and you are grateful to your body for the opportunity. Animals are smart, loving, and kind.

As you continue to move along the path, you feel strong and free, healthy and happy, glad to be here, and glad to be you. As you continue along the path, you hear the seagulls, and the ocean waves, and you feel the sun warming your head and your shoulders, you feel the breeze against your skin, as you breathe deeply and freely, filling your lungs with life-giving oxygen. You love horses, dogs, cats, bird and even smaller animals. And as you continue to move along the path, you realize that we are coming closer to the pastoral area with the barn, and you look back one more time to see this beautiful place, and to remember evermore, how wonderful and alive you feel now that you are free of the challenge that brought you here today. You love all animals and all animals love you. Animals are true friends.

As you continue to move along the path, your feet touch the gravel and as you look around, you notice the duck pond up ahead on the left and the red barn up ahead on the right. The cows are still grazing peacefully and the leaves rustle in the breeze. You see the large oak door up ahead and move forward toward it.

You arrive at the door and pull it open, the hinges squeaking again. You are now in the large round foyer with the stairs up ahead. You move toward the stairs and start up them.

Number 1

Number 2

Number 3.......Coming back.

Number 4.......Coming back.

Number 5.......Coming back slowly.......coming back.

Number 6.......Coming back to the current moment and place.....coming back.

Number 7.......Coming back...feeling rested and refreshed....coming back.

Number 8.......Coming back...feeling good, feeling fine, perfectly relaxed.

Number 9...... Coming back now, eyes open, wide awake, eyes open, wide awake.

Number 10.....Eyes open, wide awake, eyes open wide awake.

ALLERGY-FREE NOW HYPNOSIS SCRIPT

As you continue to move along the beach, you feel the sun warming the top of your head, and you feel the sea breeze against your skin, and you hear the sounds of children's laughter. To your right, you see the ocean, and the sun as it dances on the surface of the ocean. You can hear the sounds of sea gulls as they fly above the water, and as they dive into the water, happy to be alive, just like you, and as you continue to breathe deeply filling your lungs with life-giving oxygen, the colors of the children's swimsuits catch your eye... bright reds, and lemon yellows, and sky blues. You are amazed at the remarkable beauty of this place, and you feel great... happy, healthy, glad to be alive... glad to be here, and glad to be you. You feel safe in any environment. You breathe easily knowing that the environment is safe for you.

As you continue to walk along the beach, you enjoy feeling healthy and whole; you realize that this magical place has

caused a complete transformation for you. You realize that you have left behind the concern that brought you here today. Your body loves the forest, the beach and the mountains. You feel free, and healthy, and strong, as you move along the beach. You breathe deeply, filling your lungs with life-giving oxygen, and as you move along the beach, you notice that your clothes are a little looser, and you feel that you are releasing an extra few pounds in the process of leaving this challenge behind you. Your body love inside air and outside air. All air is safe for you to breathe.

As you continue to move along the beach, you notice a large group of people ahead on your right. These people are active, and happy, playing with a beach ball while others are playing volleyball. These people are active, trim, and happy, and as you observe these people, you realize that you are healthy and happy too. You breathe deeply as you walk along, and as you do, you feel your youth returning, and your breath deepening, and you feel grateful to be here, and happy to be you. You marvel at your body's ability to easily and effortlessly leave behind the concern that brought you here today. You believe that the air in the world is clean and safe to breathe, and so you breathe easily.

As you continue along the beach, you breathe deeply and easily. You feel your clothes growing looser on your body, as your metabolism adjusts favorably to the changes you are making. You feel your body strengthen, and as it does, your metabolism improves, in fact, your entire body responds favorably to these changes. You love to touch things, to eat all sorts of food, and to breathe freely without any concern. Doing so gives you pleasure. Your body is healthy and you are grateful for that.

You realize that it is time to return back the way you came, and you turn on the beach, heading back toward the path. You wave to your new friends, still playing and laughing and expressing all the health and well-being they enjoy, and you feel grateful to be a part of that group of healthy and happy people. You love all kinds of food and all food agrees with you.

You realize you are almost completely free of the challenge that brought you here today, and that you no longer have concerns about air quality or foods that might have been an issue before. You know that you live in a clean and safe world. You realize you have been given a second chance at complete health and happiness, and you are grateful to your body for the opportunity. You are strong and healthy.

As you continue to move along the path, you feel strong and free, healthy and happy, glad to be here, and glad to be you. As you continue along the path, you hear the seagulls, and the ocean waves, and you feel the sun warming your head and your shoulders, you feel the breeze against your skin, as you breathe deeply and freely, filling your lungs with life-giving oxygen. Your body easily tolerates new foods, new smells and new environments. And as you continue to move along the path, you realize that we are coming closer to the pastoral area with the barn, and you look back one more time to see this beautiful place, and to remember evermore, how wonderful and alive you feel now that you are free of the challenge that brought you here today. You love being a healthy person.

As you continue to move along the path, your feet touch the gravel and as you look around, you notice the duck pond up ahead on the left and the red barn up ahead on the right. The cows are still grazing peacefully and the leaves rustle in the breeze. You see the large oak door up ahead and move forward toward it.

You arrive at the door and pull it open, the hinges squeaking again. You are now in the large round foyer with the stairs up ahead. You move toward the stairs and start up them.

Number 1

Number 2

Number 3.......Coming back.

Number 4.......Coming back.

Number 5.......Coming back slowly.......coming back.

Number 6.......Coming back to the current moment and place.....coming back.

Number 7.......Coming back...feeling rested and refreshed....coming back.

Number 8.......Coming back...feeling good, feeling fine, perfectly relaxed.

Number 9...... Coming back now, eyes open, wide awake, eyes open, wide awake.

Number 10.....Eyes open, wide awake, eyes open wide awake.

I AM A GENIUS HYPNOSIS SCRIPT

As you continue to move along the beach, you feel the sun warming the top of your head, and you feel the sea breeze against your skin, and you hear the sounds of children's laughter. To your right, you see the ocean, and the sun as it dances on the surface of the ocean. You can hear the sounds of sea gulls as they fly above the water, and as they dive into the water, happy to be alive, just like you, and as you continue to breathe deeply filling your lungs with life-giving oxygen, the colors of the children's swimsuits catch your eye... bright reds, and lemon yellows, and sky blues. You are amazed at the remarkable beauty of this place, and you feel great... happy, healthy, glad to be alive... glad to be here, and glad to be you. You are a genius; everyone says so.

As you continue to walk along the beach, you enjoy feeling healthy and whole; you realize that this magical place has caused a complete transformation for you. You realize that

you have left behind the concern that brought you here today. Your mind is infinite in its ability to understand everything. You feel free, and healthy, and strong, as you move along the beach. You breathe deeply, filling your lungs with life-giving oxygen, and as you move along the beach, you notice that your clothes are a little looser, and you feel that you are releasing an extra few pounds in the process of leaving this concern behind you. You love to exercise your mind with crossword puzzles and other brain games. They are easy for you to complete, but they are still fun.

As you continue to move along the beach, you notice a large group of people ahead on your right. These people are active, and happy, playing with a beach ball while others are playing volleyball. These people are active, trim, and happy, and as you observe these people, you take in all the small details. Their happiness is obvious to you. You breathe deeply as you walk along, and as you do, you feel your youth returning, and your breath deepening, and you feel grateful to be here, and happy to be you. You marvel at your body's ability to easily and effortlessly leave behind the challenge that brought you here today. You love to read and you love to learn new things. Using your mind is a deep and abiding pleasure for you. You are grateful for your genius brain.

As you continue along the beach, you breathe deeply and easily. You feel your clothes growing looser on your body, as your metabolism adjusts favorably to the changes you are making. You feel your body strengthen, and as it does, your metabolism improves, in fact, your entire body responds favorably to these changes. You love to feed your brain by reading and learning new things.

You realize that it is time to return back the way you came, and you turn around on the beach, heading back toward the path. You wave to your new friends, still playing and laughing and expressing all the health and well-being they enjoy, and you feel grateful to be part of that group of healthy, smart and happy people. You love to feed your brain by reading and learning; it's really fun for you.

You realize you are completely free of the concern that brought you here today, and that you are grateful for your spectacular mind. You realize you have been given a second chance at complete health and happiness, and you are grateful to your mind and body for the opportunity. You love to think. You love to turn ideas around in your mind.

As you continue to move along the path, you feel strong and free, healthy and happy, glad to be here, and glad to be you. As you continue along the path, you hear the seagulls, and the ocean waves, and you feel the sun warming your head and your shoulders, you feel the breeze against your skin, as you breathe deeply and freely, filling your lungs with life-giving oxygen. You know that your mind is capable of understanding everything. You feed your brain by using it constantly. And as you continue to move along the path, you realize that we are coming closer to the pastoral area with the barn, and you look back one more time to see this beautiful place, and to remember evermore, how wonderful and alive you feel now that you are free of the challenge that brought you here today. Your mind is one of your favorite toys. Thinking, writing and creating are fun for you. You use your mind judiciously.

As you continue to move along the path, your feet touch the gravel and as you look around, you notice the duck pond up ahead on the left and the red barn up ahead on the right. The cows are still grazing peacefully and the leaves rustle in the breeze. You see the large oak door up ahead and move forward toward it.

You arrive at the door and pull it open, the hinges squeaking again. You are now in the large round foyer with the stairs up ahead. You move toward the stairs and start up them.

Number 1

Number 2

Number 3.......Coming back.

Number 4.......Coming back.

Number 5.......Coming back slowly.......coming back.

Number 6.......Coming back to the current moment and place.....coming back.

Number 7.......Coming back...feeling rested and refreshed....coming back.

Number 8.......Coming back...feeling good, feeling fine, perfectly relaxed.

Number 9...... Coming back now, eyes open, wide awake, eyes open, wide awake.

Number 10.....Eyes open, wide awake, eyes open wide awake.

I AM FEARLESS HYPNOSIS SCRIPT

As you continue to move along the beach, you feel the sun warming the top of your head, and you feel the sea breeze against your skin, and you hear the sounds of children's laughter. To your right, you see the ocean, and the sun as it dances on the surface of the ocean. You can hear the sounds of sea gulls as they fly above the water, and as they dive into the water, happy to be alive, just like you, and as you continue to breathe deeply filling your lungs with life-giving oxygen, the colors of the children's swimsuits catch your eye... bright reds, and lemon yellows, and sky blues. You are amazed at the remarkable beauty of this place, and you feel great... happy, healthy, glad to be alive... glad to be here, and glad to be you. You are a very courageous person. Everyone says so.

As you continue to walk along the beach, you enjoy feeling healthy and whole; you realize that this magical place has caused a complete transformation for you. You realize that

you have left behind the concerns that brought you here today. You are strong, smart and good. You feel free, and healthy, and strong, as you move along the beach. You breathe deeply, filling your lungs with life-giving oxygen, and as you move along the beach, you notice that your clothes are a little looser. You feel that you are releasing an extra few pounds in the process of leaving this challenge behind you. You love a challenge and have the confidence that you can win any competition you set your mind to win.

As you continue to move along the beach, you notice a large group of people ahead on your right. These people are active, and happy, playing with a beach ball while others are playing volleyball. These people are active, trim, and happy, and as you observe these people, you realize how much fun these teams are having competing with each other; you love competition. You breathe deeply as you walk along, and as you do, you feel your youth returning, and your breath deepening, and you feel grateful to be here, and happy to be you. You marvel at your mind and body's ability to easily and effortlessly leave behind the challenge that brought you here today. You are physically, emotionally and mental strong.

As you continue along the beach, you breathe deeply and easily. You feel your clothes growing looser on your body, as your metabolism adjusts favorably to the changes you are making. You feel your body strengthen, and as it does, your metabolism improves, in fact, your entire body responds favorably to these changes. You are a natural competitor. You fearlessly take on any challenge that interests you. You love being a courageous person.

You realize that it is time to return back the way you came, and you turn around on the beach, heading back toward the path, and you wave at your new friends, still playing and laughing and expressing all the health and well-being they enjoy. You feel grateful to be a part of that group of healthy and happy people. You love to win and strive to do so whenever the opportunity presents itself.

You realize you are completely free of the concern that brought you here today. You realize you have been given a second chance at complete health and happiness, and you are grateful to your body for the opportunity. You consider yourself a force for good.

As you continue to move along the path, you feel strong and free, healthy and happy, glad to be here, and glad to be you. As you continue along the path, you hear the seagulls, and the ocean waves, and you feel the sun warming your head and your shoulders, you feel the breeze against your skin, as you breathe deeply and freely, filling your lungs with life-giving oxygen. You are unafraid when you encounter new situations. And as you continue to move along the path, you realize that we are coming closer to the pastoral area with the barn, and you look back one more time to see this beautiful place, and to remember evermore, how wonderful and alive you feel now that you are free of the challenge that brought you here today. You are a very courageous person; the new and unfamiliar is a great and enjoyable opportunity for you to explore.

As you continue to move along the path, your feet touch the gravel and as you look around, you notice the duck pond up ahead on the left and the red barn up ahead on the right. The cows are still grazing peacefully and the leaves rustle in the breeze. You see the large oak door up ahead and move forward toward it.

You arrive at the door and pull it open, the hinges squeaking again. You are now in the large round foyer with the stairs up ahead. You move toward the stairs and start to move up them.

Number 1

Number 2

Number 3.......Coming back.

Number 4.......Coming back.

Number 5.......Coming back slowly.......coming back.

Number 6.......Coming back to the current moment and place.....coming back.

Number 7.......Coming back...feeling rested and refreshed....coming back.

Number 8.......Coming back...feeling good, feeling fine, perfectly relaxed.

Number 9...... Coming back now, eyes open, wide awake, eyes open, wide awake.

Number 10.....Eyes open, wide awake, eyes open wide awake.

I GET ALONG WITH EVERYONE HYPNOSIS SCRIPT

As you continue to move along the beach, you feel the sun warming the top of your head, and you feel the sea breeze against your skin, and you hear the sounds of children's laughter. To your right, you see the ocean, and the sun as it dances on the surface of the ocean. You can hear the sounds of sea gulls as they fly above the water, and as they dive into the water, happy to be alive, just like you, and as you continue to breathe deeply filling your lungs with life-giving oxygen, the colors of the children's swimsuits catch your eye... bright reds, and lemon yellows, and sky blues. You are amazed at the remarkable beauty of this place, and you feel great... happy, healthy, glad to be alive... glad to be here, and glad to be you. People like you and you like people. You love spending time with other people.

As you continue to walk along the beach, you enjoy feeling healthy and whole; you realize that this magical place has

caused a complete transformation in you. You realize that you have left behind the concern that brought you here today. You enjoy being with people. You feel free, and healthy, and strong, as you move along the beach. You breathe deeply, filling your lungs with life-giving oxygen, and as you move along the beach, you notice that your clothes are a little loose, and you feel that you are releasing an extra few pounds in the process of leaving this habit behind you. You really like people and you enjoy being with them.

As you continue to move along the beach, you notice a large group of people ahead on your right. These people are active, and happy, playing with a beach ball while others are playing volleyball. These people are active, trim, and happy, and as you observe these people, you feel very tempted to join them, but you content yourself with a friendly wave. You breathe deeply as you walk along, and as you do, you feel your youth returning, and your breath deepening, and you feel grateful to be here, and happy to be you. You marvel at your mind and body's ability to easily and effortlessly leave behind the concern that brought you here today. You love meeting new people in any social situation. You really love people and being with other people is your favorite thing.

As you continue along the beach, you breathe deeply and easily. You feel your clothes growing looser on your body, as your metabolism adjusts favorably to the changes you are making. You feel your body strengthen, and as it does, your metabolism improves, in fact, your entire body responds favorably to these changes. You go out of your way to meet new people. You love to be in a new situation with new people.

You realize that it is time to return back the way you came, and you turn around on the beach, heading back toward the path. You wave at your new friends, still playing and laughing and expressing all the health and well-being they enjoy, and you feel grateful to be a part of that group of healthy and happy people. You are easy going and easy to get to know. Everyone says how welcoming you are.

You realize you are completely free of the challenge that brought you here today. You realize you have been given a second chance at complete health and happiness, and you are grateful to your mind and body for the opportunity. You are happiest when you are happily interacting with other people. You are a happy, friendly person.

As you continue to move along the path, you feel strong and free, healthy and happy, glad to be here, and glad to be you. As you continue along the path, you hear the seagulls, and the ocean waves, and you feel the sun warming your head and your shoulders, you feel the breeze against your skin, as you breathe deeply and freely, filling your lungs with life-giving oxygen. You are a friendly sort of person and others sense that. And as you continue to move along the path, you realize that we are coming closer to the pastoral area with the barn, and you look back one more time to see this beautiful place, and to remember evermore, how wonderful and alive you feel now that you are free of the challenge that brought you here today. You believe that everyone in the world is either a friend or a future friend.

As you continue to move along the path, your feet touch the gravel and as you look around, you notice the duck pond up ahead on the left and the red barn up ahead on the right. The cows are still grazing peacefully and the leaves rustle in the breeze. You see the large oak door up ahead and move forward toward it.

You arrive at the door and pull it open, the hinges squeaking again. You are now in the large round foyer with the stairs up ahead. You move toward the stairs and start moving up them.

Number 1

Number 2

Number 3.......Coming back.

Number 4.......Coming back.

Number 5.......Coming back slowly.......coming back.

Number 6.......Coming back to the current moment and place.....coming back.

Number 7.......Coming back...feeling rested and refreshed....coming back.

Number 8.......Coming back...feeling good, feeling fine, perfectly relaxed.

Number 9...... Coming back now, eyes open, wide awake, eyes open, wide awake.

Number 10.....Eyes open, wide awake, eyes open wide awake.

IRRESISTIBLE ME HYPNOSIS SCRIPT

As you continue to move along the beach, you feel the sun warming the top of your head, and you feel the sea breeze against your skin, and you hear the sounds of children's laughter. To your right, you see the ocean, and the sun as it dances on the surface of the ocean. You can hear the sounds of sea gulls as they fly above the water, and as they dive into the water, happy to be alive, just like you, and as you continue to breathe deeply filling your lungs with life-giving oxygen, the colors of the children's swimsuits catch your eye... bright reds, and lemon yellows, and sky blues. You are amazed at the remarkable beauty of this place, and you feel great... happy, healthy, glad to be alive... glad to be here, and glad to be you. You are a very attractive person and everyone you encounter seems to like you a lot. You are disarmingly charming and others are drawn to you.

As you continue to walk along the beach, you enjoy feeling healthy and whole; you realize that this magical place has

caused a complete transformation for you. You realize that you have left behind the habit that brought you here today. Everyone likes you and most people find you positively irresistible. You feel free, and healthy, and strong, as you move along the beach. You breathe deeply, filling your lungs with life-giving oxygen, and as you move along the beach, you notice that your clothes are a little looser, and you feel that you are releasing an extra few pounds in the process of leaving this concern behind you. You love yourself, so naturally others find you irresistible.

As you continue to move along the beach, you notice a large group of people ahead on your right. These people are active, and happy, playing with a beach ball while others are playing volleyball. These people are active, trim, and happy. You breathe deeply as you walk along, and as you do, you feel your youth returning, and your breath deepening, and you feel grateful to be here, and happy to be you. You marvel at your mind and body's ability to easily and effortlessly leave behind the concern that brought you here today. Everyone always likes you and finds you attractive, even irresistible. You have a natural charm that is hard to ignore.

As you continue along the beach, you breathe deeply and easily. You feel your clothes growing looser on your body, as your metabolism adjusts favorably to the changes you are making. You feel your body strengthen, and as it does, your metabolism improves, in fact, your entire body responds favorably to these changes. In every social situation, people approach you in a friendly way, wanting to get to know you better.

You realize that it is time to return, and you turn around on the beach, heading back toward the path. You wave to your new friends, still playing and laughing and expressing all the health and well-being they enjoy. You feel grateful to be a part of that group of healthy and happy people. Both women and men like you and find you attractive. You exude self confidence, knowing that you are irresistible to others.

You realize you are completely free of the concern that brought you here today. You realize you have been given a second chance at complete health and happiness, and you are grateful to your body for the opportunity. It's easy for you to meet new people since you are so outgoing and confident of your appeal. It's also easy for you to get an invitation to go out with friends as well as from the new people you run into while you are out socializing.

As you continue to move along the path, you feel strong and free, healthy and happy, glad to be here, and glad to be you. As you continue along the path, you hear the seagulls, and the ocean waves rushing to shore. You feel the sun warming your head and your shoulders and you feel the breeze against your skin, as you breathe deeply and freely, filling your lungs with life-giving oxygen. You love the challenge of attracting exactly the person you want to attract in any crowd. And as you continue to move along the path, you realize that we are coming closer to the pastoral area with the barn, and you look back one more time to see this beautiful place, and to remember evermore, how wonderful and alive you feel now that you are free of the challenge that brought you here today. You are lucky to be so attractive to others and you are grateful that you are.

As you continue to move along the path, your feet touch the gravel and as you look around, you notice the duck pond up ahead on the left and the red barn up ahead on the right. The cows are still grazing peacefully and the leaves rustle in the breeze. You see the large oak door up ahead and move forward toward it.

You arrive at the door and pull it open, the hinges squeaking again. You are now in the large round foyer with the stairs up ahead. You move toward the stairs and start to move up them.

Number 1

Number 2

Number 3.......Coming back.

Number 4.......Coming back.

Number 5.......Coming back slowly.......coming back.

Number 6.......Coming back to the current moment and place.....coming back.

Number 7.......Coming back...feeling rested and refreshed....coming back.

Number 8.......Coming back...feeling good, feeling fine, perfectly relaxed.

Number 9...... Coming back now, eyes open, wide awake, eyes open, wide awake.

Number 10.....Eyes open, wide awake, eyes open wide awake.

I BREATHE EASILY HYPNOSIS SCRIPT

As you continue to move along the beach, you feel the sun warming the top of your head, and you feel the sea breeze against your skin, and you hear the sounds of children's laughter. To your right, you see the ocean, and the sun as it dances on the surface of the ocean. You can hear the sounds of sea gulls as they fly above the water, and as they dive into the water, happy to be alive, just like you; and as you continue to breathe deeply filling your lungs with life-giving oxygen, the colors of the children's swimsuits catch your eye... bright reds, and lemon yellows, and sky blues. You are amazed at the remarkable beauty of this place, and you feel great... happy, healthy, glad to be alive... glad to be here, and glad to be you. You know that oxygen is plentiful and everywhere for you to breathe. You know that there is much more oxygen in the air that you could ever use.

As you continue to walk along the beach, you enjoy feeling healthy and whole; you realize that this magical place has caused a complete transformation for you. You realize that you have left behind the challenge that brought you here today. You breathe easily and effortlessly. You feel free, and healthy, and strong, as you move along the beach. You breathe deeply, filling your lungs with life-giving oxygen, and as you move along the beach, you notice that your clothes are a little looser, and you feel that you are releasing an extra few pounds in the process of leaving this challenge behind you. You love oxygen and know that there is plenty for everyone, including you. Breathing is easy for you. You relax at the thought of breathing deeply.

As you continue to move along the beach, you notice a large group of people ahead on your right. These people are active, and happy, playing with a beach ball while others are playing volleyball. These people are active, trim, and happy. You breathe deeply as you walk along, and as you do, you feel your youth returning, and your breath deepening, and you feel grateful to be here, and happy to be you. You marvel at your mind and body's ability to easily and effortlessly leave behind the challenge that brought you here today. You love yourself and know that you deserve as much oxygen as you want.

As you continue along the beach, you breathe deeply and easily. You feel your clothes growing loose on your body, as your metabolism adjusts favorably to the changes you are making. You feel your body strengthen, and as it does, your metabolism improves, in fact, your entire body responds favorably to these changes. You are safe in the world and safe enough to breathe easily.

You realize that it is time to return the way you came, and you turn on the beach, heading back toward the path, and you wave at your new friends, still playing and laughing and expressing all the health and well-being they enjoy, and you feel grateful to be a part of that group of healthy and happy people. You know that oxygen sustains your body, so you take in a lot of it.

You realize you are completely free of the concern that brought you here today. You realize you have been given a second chance at complete health and happiness, and you are grateful to your mind and body for the opportunity. The air is clean and the world is a safe place in which to be.

As you continue to move along the path, you feel strong and free, healthy and happy, glad to be here, and glad to be you. As you continue along the path, you hear the seagulls, and the ocean waves, and you feel the sun warming your head and your shoulders, you feel the breeze against your skin, as you breathe deeply and freely, filling your lungs with life-giving oxygen. You expand your lungs joyfully to take in lots of air. And as you continue to move along the path, you realize that we are coming closer to the pastoral area with the barn, and you look back one more time to see this beautiful place, and to remember evermore, how wonderful and alive you feel now that you are free of the concern that brought you here today. Breathing is the easiest and the most natural thing in the world.

As you continue to move along the path, your feet touch the gravel and as you look around, you notice the duck pond up ahead on the left and the red barn up ahead on the right. The cows are still grazing peacefully and the leaves rustle in the breeze. You see the large oak door up ahead and move forward toward it.

You arrive at the door and pull it open, the hinges squeaking again. You are now in the large round foyer with the stairs up ahead. You move toward the stairs and start to move up them.

Number 1

Number 2

Number 3.......Coming back.

Number 4.......Coming back.

Number 5.......Coming back slowly.......coming back.

Number 6.......Coming back to the current moment and place.....coming back.

Number 7.......Coming back...feeling rested and refreshed....coming back.

Number 8.......Coming back...feeling good, feeling fine, perfectly relaxed.

Number 9...... Coming back now, eyes open, wide awake, eyes open, wide awake.

Number 10.....Eyes open, wide awake, eyes open wide awake.

I LOVE MYSELF HYPNOSIS SCRIPT

As you continue to move along the beach, you feel the sun warming the top of your head, and you feel the sea breeze against your skin, and you hear the sounds of children's laughter. To your right, you see the ocean, and the sun as it dances on the surface of the ocean. You can hear the sounds of sea gulls as they fly above the water, and as they dive into the water, happy to be alive, just like you, and as you continue to breathe deeply filling your lungs with life-giving oxygen, the colors of the children's swimsuits catch your eye... bright reds, and lemon yellows, and sky blues. You are amazed at the remarkable beauty of this place, and you feel great... happy, healthy, glad to be alive... glad to be here, and glad to be you. You love yourself, naturally. You're a good and kind person.

As you continue to walk along the beach, you enjoy feeling healthy and whole; you realize that this magical place has caused a complete transformation for you. You realize that

you have left behind the challenge that brought you here today. You are a good person; everyone likes you. You feel free, and healthy, and strong, as you move along the beach. You breathe deeply, filling your lungs with life-giving oxygen, and as you move along the beach, you notice that your clothes are a little loose, and you feel that you are releasing an extra few pounds in the process of leaving this concern behind. You care about other people and you are kind to everyone you encounter. You are infinitely lovable.

As you continue to move along the beach, you notice a large group of people ahead on your right. These people are active, and happy, playing with a beach ball while others are playing volleyball. These people are active, trim, and happy, and as you observe these people, you notice them waving to you. You feel happy to be the recipient of such acceptance and welcome. You breathe deeply as you walk along, and as you do, you feel your youth returning, and your breath deepening, and you feel grateful to be here, and happy to be you. You marvel at your body's ability to easily and effortlessly leave behind the habit that brought you here today. You are happy with your appearance and you take care of yourself. Being good to yourself makes total sense.

As you continue along the beach, you breathe deeply and easily. You feel your clothes growing looser on your body, as your metabolism adjusts favorably to the changes you are making. You feel your body strengthen, and as it does, your metabolism improves, in fact, your entire body responds favorably to these changes. You are deserving of kindness from others and you get it. You are also kind to yourself.

You realize that it is time to return back the way you came, and you turn around on the beach, heading back toward the path. You wave to your new friends, still playing and laughing and expressing all the health and well-being they enjoy. You feel grateful to be a part of that group of healthy and happy people. You expect to be treated respectfully and you are.

You realize you are completely free of the challenge that brought you here today. You realize you have been given a second chance at complete health and happiness, and you are grateful to your mind and body for the opportunity. You are as kind to yourself as you are to others.

As you continue to move along the path, you feel strong and free, healthy and happy, glad to be here, and glad to be you. As you continue along the path, you hear the seagulls, and the ocean waves, and you feel the sun warming your head and your shoulders, you feel the breeze against your skin, as you breathe deeply and freely, filling your lungs with life-giving oxygen. You love yourself because you are a good person. And as you continue to move along the path, you realize that we are coming closer to the pastoral area with the barn, and you look back one more time to see this beautiful place, and to remember evermore, how wonderful and alive you feel now that you are free of the challenge that brought you here today. You are happy to be you, to be alive and to be here.

As you continue to move along the path, your feet touch the gravel and as you look around, you notice the duck pond up ahead on the left and the red barn up ahead on the right. The cows are still grazing peacefully and the leaves rustle in the breeze. You see the large oak door up ahead and move forward toward it.

You arrive at the door and pull it open, the hinges squeaking again. You are now in the large round foyer with the stairs up ahead. You move toward the stairs and start to move up them.

Number 1

Number 2

Number 3.......Coming back.

Number 4.......Coming back.

Number 5.......Coming back slowly.......coming back.

Number 6.......Coming back to the current moment and place.....coming back.

Number 7.......Coming back...feeling rested and refreshed....coming back.

Number 8.......Coming back...feeling good, feeling fine, perfectly relaxed.

Number 9...... Coming back now, eyes open, wide awake, eyes open, wide awake.

Number 10.....Eyes open, wide awake, eyes open wide awake.

I AM A HAPPY PERSON HYPNOSIS SCRIPT

As you continue to move along the beach, you feel the sun warming the top of your head, and you feel the sea breeze against your skin, and you hear the sounds of children's laughter. To your right, you see the ocean, and the sun as it dances on the surface of the water. You can hear the sounds of sea gulls as they fly above the water, and as they dive into the water, happy to be alive, just like you, and as you continue to breathe deeply filling your lungs with life-giving oxygen, the colors of the children's swimsuits catch your eye... bright reds, and lemon yellows, and sky blues. You are amazed at the remarkable beauty of this place, and you feel great... happy, healthy, glad to be alive... glad to be here, and glad to be you. You are a happy person.

As you continue to walk along the beach, you enjoy feeling healthy and whole; you realize that this magical place has caused a complete transformation for you. You realize that you have left behind the concern that brought you here today. You laugh because you are happy. You feel free, and healthy, and strong, as you move along the beach. You breathe deeply, filling your lungs with life-giving oxygen, and as you move along the beach, you notice that your clothes are a little looser, and you feel that you are releasing an extra few pounds in the process of leaving this challenge behind you. Your happiness spills out of you onto other people, drawing them closer to you. You are a happy person.

As you continue to move along the beach, you notice a large group of people ahead on your right. These people are active, and happy, playing with a beach ball while others are playing volleyball. These people are active, trim, and happy, and as you observe these people, you feel as happy as they seem. You breathe deeply as you walk along, and as you do, you feel your youth returning, and your breath deepening, and you feel grateful to be here, and happy to be you. You marvel at your mind and body's ability to easily and effortlessly leave behind the concern that brought you here today. You have a smile for everyone you meet.

As you continue along the beach, you breathe deeply and easily. You feel your clothes growing loose on your body, as your metabolism adjusts favorably to the changes you are making. You feel your body strengthen, and as it does, your metabolism improves, in fact, your entire body responds favorably to these changes. You are easily amused, so you laugh easily.

You realize that it is time to return back the way you came, and you turn around on the beach, heading back toward the path. You wave at your new friends, still playing and laughing and expressing all the health and well-being they enjoy, and you feel grateful to be a part of that group of healthy and happy people. You really like yourself and you even laugh at your own jokes sometimes.

You realize you are completely free of the challenge that brought you here today, and that you no longer desire to do anything that is counter-productive to your happiness. You realize you have been given a second chance at complete health and happiness, and you are grateful to your mind and body for the opportunity. You are a generous person and you share your happiness with others.

As you continue to move along the path, you feel strong and free, healthy and happy, glad to be here, and glad to be you. As you continue along the path, you hear the seagulls, and the ocean waves, and you feel the sun warming your head and your shoulders, you feel the breeze against your skin, as you breathe deeply and freely, filling your lungs with life-giving oxygen. You are kind to everyone and that makes you happy. And as you continue to move along the path, you realize that we are coming closer to the pastoral area with the barn, and you look back one more time to see this beautiful place, and to remember evermore, how wonderful and alive you feel now that you are free of the challenge that brought you here today. You are one of the most cheerful people you know.

As you continue to move along the path, your feet touch the gravel and as you look around, you notice the duck pond up ahead on the left and the red barn up ahead on the right. The cows are still grazing peacefully and the leaves rustle in the breeze. You see the large oak door up ahead and move forward toward it.

You arrive at the door and pull it open, the hinges squeaking again. You are now in the large round foyer with the stairs up ahead. You head toward the stairs and start to move up them.

Number 1

Number 2

Number 3.......Coming back.

Number 4.......Coming back.

Number 5.......Coming back slowly.......coming back.

Number 6.......Coming back to the current moment and place.....coming back.

Number 7.......Coming back...feeling rested and refreshed....coming back.

Number 8.......Coming back...feeling good, feeling fine, perfectly relaxed.

Number 9...... Coming back now, eyes open, wide awake, eyes open, wide awake.

Number 10.....Eyes open, wide awake, eyes open wide awake.

I LIVE IN A SAFE WORLD HYPNOSIS SCRIPT

As you continue to move along the beach, you feel the sun warming the top of your head, and you feel the sea breeze against your skin, and you hear the sounds of children's laughter. To your right, you see the ocean, and the sun as it dances on the surface of the ocean. You can hear the sounds of sea gulls as they fly above the water, and as they dive into the water, happy to be alive, just like you, and as you continue to breathe deeply filling your lungs with life-giving oxygen, the colors of the children's swimsuits catch your eye... bright reds, and lemon yellows, and sky blues. You are amazed at the remarkable beauty of this place, and you feel great... happy, healthy, glad to be alive... glad to be here, and glad to be you. You are safe in the world. You live in a good place surrounded by good people. Your safety is assured.

As you continue to walk along the beach, you enjoy feeling healthy and whole; you realize that this magical place has

caused a complete transformation for you. You realize that you have left behind the concern that brought you here today. You are always protected. You feel free, and healthy, and strong, as you move along the beach. You breathe deeply, filling your lungs with life-giving oxygen, and as you move along the beach, you notice that your clothes are a little loose, and you feel that you are releasing an extra few pounds in the process of leaving this concern behind you. Safety is with you at all times. You are always safe in any situation. You attract only safe happenings.

As you continue to move along the beach, you notice a large group of people ahead on your right. These people are active, and happy, playing with a beach ball while others are playing volleyball. These people are active, trim, and happy, and as you observe these people you sense in them, their safety and you take that on as your own. You breathe deeply as you walk along, and as you do, you feel your youth returning, and your breath deepening, and you feel grateful to be here, and happy to be you. You marvel at your mind and body's ability to easily and effortlessly leave behind the challenge that brought you here today. You live in a world that is safe and good.

As you continue along the beach, you breathe deeply and easily. You feel your clothes growing loose on your body, as your metabolism adjusts favorably to the changes you are making. You feel your body strengthen, and as it does, your metabolism improves, in fact, your entire body responds favorably to these changes. You are surrounded by people you trust. You trust others easily and you attract only trustworthy people into your life.

You realize that it is time to return back the way you came, and you turn on the beach, heading back toward the path, and you wave at your new friends, still playing and laughing and expressing all the health and well-being they enjoy. You feel grateful to be a part of that group of healthy, safe and happy people. When you are at home you feel safe, and when you are out, you feel safe. Safety is always with you.

You realize you are completely free of the challenge that brought you here today, and that you no longer have a concern about your safety.. You realize you have been given a second chance at complete health and happiness, and you are grateful to your body for the opportunity. Safety is the norm; it's only natural to be safe. If there is anything other than a safe situation near you, you sense it and retreat to a safer place.

As you continue to move along the path, you feel strong and free, healthy and happy, glad to be here, and glad to be you. As you continue along the path, you hear the seagulls, and the ocean waves, and you feel the sun warming your head and your shoulders, you feel the breeze against your skin, as you breathe deeply and freely, filling your lungs with life-giving oxygen. You are always safe in every situation. And as you continue to move along the path, you realize that we are coming closer to the pastoral area with the barn, and you look back one more time to see this beautiful place, and to remember evermore, how wonderful and alive you feel now that you are free of the challenge that brought you here today. You feel that you always have an angel on your shoulder.

As you continue to move along the path, your feet touch the gravel and as you look around, you notice the duck pond up ahead on the left and the red barn up ahead on the right. The cows are still grazing peacefully and the leaves rustle in the breeze. You see the large oak door up ahead and move forward toward it.

You arrive at the door and pull it open, the hinges squeaking again. You are now in the large round foyer with the stairs up ahead. You move toward the stairs and start to move up them.

Number 1

Number 2

Number 3.......Coming back.

Number 4.......Coming back.

Number 5.......Coming back slowly.......coming back.

Number 6.......Coming back to the current moment and place.....coming back.

Number 7.......Coming back...feeling rested and refreshed....coming back.

Number 8.......Coming back...feeling good, feeling fine, perfectly relaxed.

Number 9...... Coming back now, eyes open, wide awake, eyes open, wide awake.

Number 10.....Eyes open, wide awake, eyes open wide awake.

I AM POPULAR HYPNOSIS SCRIPT

As you continue to move along the beach, you feel the sun warming the top of your head, and you feel the sea breeze against your skin, and you hear the sounds of children's laughter. To your right, you see the ocean, and the sun as it dances on the surface of the ocean. You can hear the sounds of sea gulls as they fly above the water, and as they dive into the water, happy to be alive, just like you, and as you continue to breathe deeply filling your lungs with life-giving oxygen, the colors of the children's swimsuits catch your eye... bright reds, and lemon yellows, and sky blues. You are amazed at the remarkable beauty of this place, and you feel great... happy, healthy, glad to be alive... glad to be here, and glad to be you. Everyone likes you.

As you continue to walk along the beach, you enjoy feeling healthy and whole; you realize that this magical place has caused a complete transformation for you. You realize that you have left behind the concern that brought you here today. You enjoy people so much, being with them, interacting with them and getting to know them. You feel free, and healthy, and strong, as you move along the beach. You breathe deeply, filling your lungs with life-giving oxygen, and as you move along the beach, you notice that your clothes feel a little loose, and you feel that you are releasing an extra few pounds in the process of leaving this challenge behind you. You are the life of every party.

As you continue to move along the beach, you notice a large group of people ahead on your right. These people are active, and happy, playing with a beach ball while others are playing volleyball. These people are active, trim, and happy, and as you observe these people, you feel a part of that group and happy about it. You breathe deeply as you walk along, and as you do, you feel your youth returning, and your breath deepening, and you feel grateful to be here, and happy to be you. You marvel at your body's ability to easily and effortlessly leave behind the concern that brought you here today. You are funny and happy; and you laugh at yourself unselfconsciously.

As you continue along the beach, you breathe deeply and easily. You feel your clothes growing looser on your body, as your metabolism adjusts favorably to the changes you are making. You feel your body strengthen, and as it does, your metabolism improves, in fact, your entire body responds favorably to these changes. It makes you happy to make other people feel good.

You realize that it is time to return the way you came, and you turn on the beach, heading back toward the path, and you wave at your new friends, still playing and laughing and expressing all the health and well-being they enjoy, and you feel grateful to be a part of that group of healthy and happy people. You are a great listener; you listen to others carefully and with interest.

You realize you are completely free of the concern that brought you here today. You realize you have been given a second chance at complete health and happiness, and you are grateful to your body for the opportunity. You are totally interested in what other people have to say. Everyone says what a good listener you are.

As you continue to move along the path, you feel strong and free, healthy and happy, glad to be here, and glad to be you. As you continue along the path, you hear the seagulls, and the ocean waves, and you feel the sun warming your head and your shoulders, you feel the breeze against your skin, as you breathe deeply and freely, filling your lungs with life-giving oxygen. You love to tell stories that make people laugh. And as you continue to move along the path, you realize that we are coming closer to the pastoral area with the barn, and you look back one more time to see this beautiful place, and to remember evermore, how wonderful and alive you feel now that you are free of the challenge that brought you here today. You are kind to everyone.

As you continue to move along the path, your feet touch the gravel and as you look around, you notice the duck pond up ahead on the left and the red barn up ahead on the right. The cows are still grazing peacefully and the leaves rustle in the breeze. You see the large oak door up ahead and move forward toward it.

You arrive at the door and pull it open, the hinges squeaking again. You are now in the large round foyer with the stairs up ahead. You move toward the stairs and start to move up them.

Number 1

Number 2

Number 3.......Coming back.

Number 4.......Coming back.

Number 5.......Coming back slowly.......coming back.

Number 6.......Coming back to the current moment and place.....coming back.

Number 7.......Coming back...feeling rested and refreshed....coming back.

Number 8.......Coming back...feeling good, feeling fine, perfectly relaxed.

Number 9...... Coming back now, eyes open, wide awake, eyes open, wide awake.

Number 10.....Eyes open, wide awake, eyes open wide awake.

I LOVE LIFE HYPNOSIS SCRIPT

As you continue to move along the beach, you feel the sun warming the top of your head, and you feel the sea breeze against your skin, and you hear the sounds of children's laughter. To your right, you see the ocean, and the sun as it dances on the surface of the ocean. You can hear the sounds of sea gulls as they fly above the water, and as they dive into the water, happy to be alive, just like you, and as you continue to breathe deeply filling your lungs with life-giving oxygen, the colors of the children's swimsuits catch your eye... bright reds, and lemon yellows, and sky blues. You are amazed at the remarkable beauty of this place, and you feel great... happy, healthy, glad to be alive... glad to be here, and glad to be you. You are so happy to be alive. You enjoy every day.

As you continue to walk along the beach, you enjoy feeling healthy and whole; you realize that this magical place has caused a complete transformation for you. You realize that

you have left behind the concern that brought you here today. You love life and cherish all your experiences. You feel free, and healthy, and strong, as you move along the beach. You breathe deeply, filling your lungs with life-giving oxygen, and as you move along the beach, you notice that your clothes are a little loose, and you feel that you are releasing an extra few pounds in the process of leaving this habit behind you. You love to play and have fun and you invite any opportunity to do so.

As you continue to move along the beach, you notice a larger group of people ahead on your right. These people are active, and happy, playing with a beach ball while others are playing volleyball. These people are active, trim, and happy, and as you observe these people, you feel happy to see these people having so much fun. You breathe deeply as you walk along, and as you do, you feel your youth returning, and your breath deepening, and you feel grateful to be here, and happy to be you. You marvel at your body's ability to easily and effortlessly leave behind the habit that brought you here today. You love to work at your job.

As you continue along the beach, you breathe deeply and easily. You feel your clothes growing loose on your body, as your metabolism adjusts favorably to the changes you are making. You feel your body strengthen, and as it does, your metabolism improves, in fact, your entire body responds favorably to these changes. You are lucky to engage in work that matters to you. You are so lucky to have such a great life!

You realize that it is time to return the way you came, and you turn on the beach, heading back toward the path, and you wave at your new friends, still playing and laughing and expressing all the health and well-being they enjoy, and you feel grateful to be a part of that group of healthy and happy people. You love your friends and family and you appreciate them. You feel appreciated in return. You feel blessed to be able to attract everything you want or need.

You realize you are completely free of the concern that brought you here today. You realize you have been given a second chance at complete health and happiness, and you are grateful to your body for the opportunity. You see the best in everyone and everything. You are a happy person.

As you continue to move along the path, you feel strong and free, healthy and happy, glad to be here, and glad to be you. As you continue along the path, you hear the seagulls, and the ocean waves, and you feel the sun warming your head and your shoulders, you feel the breeze against your skin, as you breathe deeply and freely, filling your lungs with life-giving oxygen. You smile almost all the time with gratitude for your great life.

And as you continue to move along the path, you realize that we are coming closer to the pastoral area with the barn, and you look back one more time to see this beautiful place, and to remember evermore, how wonderful and alive you feel now that you are free of the challenge that brought you here today. You are glad to be alive and you are glad to be you.

As you continue to move along the path, your feet touch the gravel and as you look around, you notice the duck pond up ahead on the left and the red barn up ahead on the right. The cows are still grazing peacefully and the leaves rustle in the breeze. You see the large oak door up ahead and move forward toward it.

You arrive at the door and pull it open, the hinges squeaking again. You are now in the large round foyer with the stairs up ahead. You move toward the stairs and start to move up them.

Number 1

Number 2

Number 3.......Coming back.

Number 4.......Coming back.

Number 5.......Coming back slowly.......coming back.

Number 6.......Coming back to the current moment and place.....coming back.

Number 7.......Coming back...feeling rested and refreshed....coming back.

Number 8.......Coming back...feeling good, feeling fine, perfectly relaxed.

Number 9...... Coming back now, eyes open, wide awake, eyes open, wide awake.

Number 10.....Eyes open, wide awake, eyes open wide awake.

STOP SMOKING HYPNOSIS BONUS SCRIPT

As you continue to move along the beach, you feel the sun warming the top of your head, and you feel the sea breeze against your skin, and you hear the sounds of children's laughter. To your right, you see the ocean, and the sun as it dances on the surface of the ocean. You can hear the sounds of sea gulls as they fly above the water, and as they dive into the water, happy to be alive, just like you, and as you continue to breathe deeply filling your lungs with life-giving oxygen, the colors of the children's swimsuits catch your eye... bright reds, and lemon yellows, and sky blues. You are amazed at the remarkable beauty of this place, and you feel great... happy, healthy, glad to be alive... glad to be here, and glad to be you.

As you continue to walk along the beach, you enjoy feeling healthy and whole; you realize that this magical place has caused a complete transformation for you. You realize that you have left behind the habit that brought you here today.

You feel free, and healthy, and strong, as you move along the beach. You breathe deeply, filling your lungs with life-giving oxygen, and as you move along the beach, you notice that your clothes are a little loose, and you feel that you are releasing an extra 3-5 pounds in the process of leaving this habit behind you.

And as you continue to move along the path, you notice that there are a lot of people on the beach, but there seem to be 2 distinct groups. The group on your right is a small group, and they are more somber than the rest of the people on the beach. As you move toward them, you observe them, and you try to figure out why they seem so gloomy. As you look at them, you notice first of all, that they are sitting still, looking at the ocean and not really enjoying the beach. There are just a few of them, and as you look at them, you see that they are not interacting with each other, they are just sitting there, and then you notice that they are also smoking. And you realize as you see them, that they are not enjoying this activity, it is just something that they are doing. You sense their isolation, and you feel for them.

You realize that before today, you were a lot like them, solitary and giving up a lot for a habit that wasn't really bringing you much pleasure.

As you continue to move along the beach, you notice a larger group of people ahead on your right. These people are active, and happy, playing with a beach ball while others are playing volleyball. These people are active, trim, and happy, and as you observe these people, you realize that if you had to choose the group that you now most closely resemble, it is this group of healthy, happy, active people. You breathe deeply as you walk along, and as you do, you feel your youth returning, and your breath deepening, and you feel grateful to be here, and happy to be you. You feel strong and healthy and happy as you move along the beach; someone from the active group invites you to join them in a volleyball game and you do. You are able to play well, and you feel your body growing stronger moment by moment. You thank your new friends and move along the beach path, and as you go, you marvel at your body's ability to easily and effortlessly leave behind the habit that brought you here today.

As you continue along the beach, you breathe deeply and easily. You feel your clothes growing loose on your body, as your metabolism adjusts favorably to the changes you are making. You feel your body strengthen, and as it does, your metabolism improves, in fact, your entire body responds favorably to these changes.

You realize that it is time to return the way you came, and you turn on the beach, heading back toward the path, and you wave at your new friends, still playing and laughing and expressing all the health and well-being they enjoy, and you feel grateful to be one of that group of healthy and happy people.

You realize you are completely free of the habit that brought you here today, and that you no longer desire to do anything that is unhealthy for your body. You realize you have been given a second chance at complete health, and you are grateful to your body for the opportunity.

As you continue to move along the path, you feel strong and free, healthy and happy, glad to be here, and glad to be you. As you continue along the path, you hear the seagulls, and the ocean waves, and you feel the sun warming your head and your shoulders, you feel the breeze against your skin, as you breathe deeply and freely, filling your lungs with life-giving oxygen. And as you continue to move along the path, you realize that we are coming closer to the pastoral area with the barn, and you look back one more time to see this beautiful place, and to remember evermore, how wonderful and alive you feel now that you are free of the challenge that brought you here today.

And as you continue to move along the path, you realize that we are coming closer to the pastoral area with the barn, and you look back one more time to see this beautiful place, and to remember evermore, how wonderful and alive you feel now that you are free of the challenge that brought you here today. You are glad to be alive and you are glad to be you.

As you continue to move along the path, your feet touch the gravel and as you look around, you notice the duck pond up ahead on the left and the red barn up ahead on the right. The cows are still grazing peacefully and the leaves rustle in the breeze. You see the large oak door up ahead and move forward toward it.

You arrive at the door and pull it open, the hinges squeaking again. You are now in the large round foyer with the stairs up ahead. You move toward the stairs and start to move up them.

Number 1

Number 2

Number 3.......Coming back.

Number 4.......Coming back.

Number 5.......Coming back slowly.......coming back.

Number 6.......Coming back to the current moment and place.....coming back.

Number 7.......Coming back...feeling rested and refreshed....coming back.

Number 8.......Coming back...feeling good, feeling fine, perfectly relaxed.

Number 9...... Coming back now, eyes open, wide awake, eyes open, wide awake.

Number 10.....Eyes open, wide awake, eyes open wide awake.

CHAPTER 3

HYPNOSIS PROGRAM SCRIPTS

Several Hypnosis applications are ideally suited to a series of Hypnosis scripts. Weight Loss and Stress Reduction are two big ones, so we have provided a series of 3 Hypnosis scripts for each of these applications in this chapter.

For a weight loss program, we recommend using the first session for as long as it's effective. In the case of Self Hypnosis, I've personally found that after about 3 weeks of daily sessions, it's generally time to move onto the next script. For professional use of these program scripts, use your own judgment. The length of time your client will use each script depends on how frequent your sessions are and how your client is responding to the sessions.

For personal use, the first session script should be used for about 3 weeks unless you hit a plateau before that in which case, move immediately to the second session script. That second script may work perfectly for the rest of your Self Hypnosis weight loss program, but if you have 50 or more pounds to lose, you will likely have the opportunity to use the third script too. If so, move to the third script about 3 weeks after beginning with Session Script 2.

Remember, everyone is different, so everyone experiences hypnosis a bit differently. When the scale stops registering a weight loss, you or your client are ready to progress to the next script. Interestingly, if you need another session after Session 3, you can go right back to Session 1 and use it again with full effectiveness.

For Stress Reduction, having a series is ideal because it can take up to 12 weeks for a client or yourself to regain full control of his/her physiological and emotional reactions to external stressors. Use Session Script 1 for about 2 weeks. Two weeks is generally ideal and for many individuals, using each sequential script for about 2 weeks in ideal. In both Weight Loss and Stress Reduction, the first session is the core script, so cycling back to that session after using the others is recommended.

WEIGHT MANAGEMENT SERIES OF SCRIPTS

The first series we will cover is the Weight Management Series. This series is ideally suited for an individual or client who has 30 or more pounds to lose, or someone who is in the last phase of his/her weight loss program.

As strange as it sounds, the last 10 pounds can be as challenging to a weight loss client or individual as the first 20 pounds were. This program series responds to the need for a weight loss boost when the client or you hit a weight loss plateau during your Hypnosis weight loss program. No worries; you just move on to the next script in the series.

Whether you are using these scripts for personal or professional use, follow your own judgment when deciding when to progress to the next script. Also, please feel free to modify these session scripts in any way you choose. Our goal in writing this book is to help you or your client reach your goals.

WEIGHT LOSS SESSION SCRIPT 1

As you move along the beach, you hear the sounds of the waves breaking on the shore, you hear the sounds of the sea gulls as they swoop and dive over the water's edge, and you feel the sun warming the top of your head, and you hear the sounds of children playing, as you continue to move along the beach.

As you continue to breathe deeply, filling your lungs with life-giving oxygen, you feel lighter and lighter, and you realize that you are metabolizing food more efficiently all the time; in fact, you are digesting, assimilating, and eliminating your food easily and quickly. You metabolize food like a healthy 10 year old child.

You feel lighter and lighter all the time, and you have the sense that your clothing is feeling a little loose on you. As you continue to walk along the path, you notice little children playing at the water's edge, laughing and having fun, as they throw a beach ball back and forth to each other.

As you watch them run back and forth, you realize how much fun it is, to be able to be active again. Now that you are releasing unnecessary weight, you look forward to becoming much more active. You enjoy eating food that's good for your body; in fact, the only food that interests you is healthy food.

As you continue to breathe deeply, filling your lungs with life-giving oxygen, you notice a group of people between the path and the water's edge. You see them sitting there, talking quietly to each other, and eating a lot of the foods you used to eat. And as you continue to observe them, you see that they don't look very happy, they all seem to be over-weight, and as you listen to the sounds of their voices, your sense the lack of joy and happiness in that group. And you feel for them, knowing how some of them feel... left out, unattractive, and sad. You can't help feeling grateful that you have conquered the weight challenge that brought you here today, and that you are getting thinner and thinner, moment by moment and day by day, and feeling healthier and healthier all the time. You love to eat simple, nourishing food. You even prefer fat free food these days. You are rewarded for your efforts by having more energy and a brighter, happier outlook.

As you continue to walk along the beach, you smell the saltwater, and you hear the seagulls as they swoop and dive, happy to be alive. You are happy too, and glad to be alive. You feel the sun warming your face and your shoulders, and you feel the salt breeze as it caresses you skin. You see the sun as it sparkles on the ocean, and you breathe deeply, enjoying the day and enjoying being you.

You are starting to get hungry and the only food that appeals to that hunger is chicken, fish, and fresh, green salads. Umm, your mouth is starting to water just thinking about this yummy food.

As you walk along the beach path, you enjoy the unfamiliar but pleasant sensation of being admired by others, and find now that you enjoy it when others look at you. You sense their approval of you, and you are grateful to realize that you deserve it; so, you enjoy it. You feel your shyness melting away, and you feel the joy of knowing that you are doing what you can to improve your health and your looks easily and quickly. You are pleased to realize that you don't have cravings for foods that aren't good for you, and you find yourself enjoying fish, chicken, and salads enormously. You never get tired of eating healthy food. You also realize that it takes much less food to satisfy you, and you really enjoy what you eat. You digest all the food that you eat easily and effortlessly, and you assimilate and eliminate all foods perfectly. You feel your body systems speed up to accomplish your goal of reaching your perfect weight, and maintaining it easily and effortlessly. You are grateful that your body is working with you to help you reach your goal. You feel your metabolism speed up, and you digest easily and effortlessly. You also assimilate and eliminate all food easily and quickly.

You notice as you continue to move along the beach, on the other side on the path, there is a group of very active adults... they're playing volleyball, and throwing a Frisbee, and laughing and carrying on, having a really good time.

These are very attractive, thin and healthy people, and you find yourself drawn to this group. As you continue to move along the beach, you notice a long table full of food...food that smells delicious. And as you continue to observe this table, you see that it is full of chicken, fish, salads, and fruit, and you realize that from this moment forward, only this healthy sort of food attracts you. You feel your mouth watering as you look at this food...you smell the food and you realize that you have never smelled anything that smelled so good. You are starting to realize how hungry you are.

You are definitely hungry, and as you continue to move slowly along the path, one of this group waves you over. You notice how slim and attractive the people in this group are, and you are aware of your own clothes growing looser. As you join this group, you realize that if you HAD to choose between this group and the group on the other side of the path, that this is the group that you belong with. You experience such a sense of belonging and welcome from this group as they greet you and invite you to share their food. You feel so pleased to have left behind, the challenge that brought you here today. You fill a plate with good healthy food, and wonder at your food choices before you embarked on this wonderful adventure. This food is mouthwateringly good, and you eat it with total delight.

You feel your body digesting and assimilating all the good in this food, and you feel your body begin the process of elimination as well. You are grateful that your body works so efficiently at digesting, assimilating, and eliminating all foods that you eat from this moment forward. You eat what you need to be satisfied, and you completely digest all that you eat.

As you wave goodbye to your new friends, you continue along the path and see friends and family members up ahead on the left of the path. They are applauding and cheering you for having taken control of your life and your body; you feel happy and proud to be acknowledged by your friends and family for your achievement in gaining control of your weight and your life. This day is just so perfect and wonderful, and you are so glad to be able to participate in this freeing experience. You know that you are struggle-free of the challenges that brought you here today; you realize how easy it is to create everything you want in your life, starting right here and right now. You feel as if your weight loss goal has already been reached, at least energetically. You no longer feel like the person who ate out of loneliness or boredom. You are now a person who eats to nourish his/her body, and while you enjoy eating, you understand that the purpose of eating is to fuel your body. You know that from this moment forward, you are free of cravings for any food that doesn't serve your desire for a trim and healthy body. You feel amazingly free and clear now about food and food matters.

As you move along the beach, you enjoy the feeling of the sun on your face and shoulders, and you marvel at how loose your clothes feel on you. You hear the sounds of the seagulls and the roar of the waves, as they crash to the shore, and you feel the breezes caress your skin, and you decide that from this moment forward, you are free of the challenge that brought you here today, effortlessly and easily, moment by moment and day by day.

It's so nice here at the water's edge, and it's so nice to know that you are free of the challenge that brought you here today. Its amazing how much better you feel. Your life feels full of possibility and full of options.

As you turn on the path and begin moving back the way we came, you feel grateful and happy to be the real you, not the old you hiding beneath your body armoring, and you smile with pleasure as your friends and family applaud your successful efforts to leave behind the challenges that brought you here today. You wave goodbye to them as you continue along the path.

As you continue along the path, you hear the seagulls and the ocean waves, you feel the sun warming your head and your shoulders, you feel the breeze against your skin as you breathe deeply and freely, filling your lungs with life-giving oxygen. And as you continue to move along the path, you realize that we are coming closer to the pastoral area with the barn, and you look back one more time to see this beautiful beach and to remember evermore how wonderful and alive you feel now that you are free of the challenge that brought you here today.

As you continue to move along the path, you feel strong and free, healthy and happy, glad to be here, and glad to be you. As you continue along the path, you hear the seagulls, and the ocean waves, and you feel the sun warming your head and your shoulders, you feel the breeze against your skin, as you breathe deeply and freely, filling your lungs with life-giving oxygen. And as you continue to move along the path, you realize that we are coming closer to the pastoral area with the barn, and you look back one more time to see this beautiful place, and to remember evermore, how wonderful and alive you feel now that you are free of the challenge that brought you here today.

As you continue to move along the path, your feet touch the gravel and as you look around, you notice the duck pond up ahead on the left and the red barn up ahead on the right. The cows are still grazing peacefully and the leaves rustle in the breeze. You see the large oak door up ahead and move forward toward it.

You arrive at the door and pull it open, the hinges squeaking again. You are now in the large round foyer with the stairs up ahead. You move toward the stairs and begin to move up them.

Number 1

Number 2

Number 3.......Coming back.

Number 4.......Coming back.

Number 5.......Coming back slowly.......coming back.

Number 6.......Coming back to the current moment and place.....coming back.

Number 7.......Coming back...feeling rested and refreshed....coming back.

Number 8.......Coming back...feeling good, feeling fine, perfectly relaxed.

Number 9...... Coming back now, eyes open, wide awake, eyes open, wide awake.

Number 10.....Eyes open, wide awake, eyes open wide awake.

WEIGHT LOSS SESSION SCRIPT 2

As you continue to move along the beach, you feel the sun warming the top of your head, and you feel the sea breeze against your skin, and you hear the sounds of children's laughter. To your right, you see the ocean, and the sun as it dances on the surface of the water. You can hear the sounds of sea gulls as they fly above the water, and as they dive into the water, happy to be alive, just like you, and as you continue to breathe deeply filling your lungs with life-giving oxygen, the colors of the children's swimsuits catch your eye... bright reds, and lemon yellows, and sky blues. This place is beautiful and you're happy to be here.

As you continue to walk along the beach, you enjoy feeling healthy and whole; you really enjoy that your body is slimming and you credit this beautiful place. You realize that this magical place has caused a complete transformation for you. You realize that you love your body and you want it to be healthier and even more slender. You feel free, and healthy, and strong, as you move along the beach. You breathe deeply, filling your lungs with life-giving oxygen, and as you move along the beach, you notice that your clothes are a little bit loose on you , and you can feel the excess weight leaving your body. You now eat to nourish your body, not to recreate like in the old days. Those days seem so far behind you.

As you continue to move along the beach, you notice a large group of people ahead on your right. These people are active, and happy, playing with a beach ball while others are playing volleyball. These people are active, trim, and happy, and as you observe these people, you feel a sense of oneness with them. They are clearly healthy and weight appropriate, and having the time of their lives. You know that if you choose to join their play, you could easily keep up with them and that makes you happy. You breathe deeply as you walk along, and as you do, you feel your youth returning, and your breath deepening, and you feel grateful to be here, and happy to be you. You marvel at your body's ability to easily and effortlessly leave behind the concern that brought you here today. Eating is a true pleasure but being slim, attractive and comfortable in your own skin is a greater pleasure for you. Your body is your home and you like a tidy home.

As you continue along the beach, you breathe deeply and easily. You feel your clothes growing loose on your body, as your metabolism adjusts favorably to the changes you are making. You feel your body strengthen, and as it does, your metabolism improves, in fact, your entire body responds favorably to these changes. You have decided to live by the rule that you take care of your body and your body takes care of you.

You realize that it is time to return back the way you came, and you turn around on the beach, heading back toward the path. You wave at your new friends, still playing and laughing and expressing all the health and well-being they enjoy, and you feel grateful to be a part of that group of healthy and happy people. You are also grateful that you love to eat nutritious, calorie conscious meals; happily you never feel deprived, only happy with your healthy attitude toward food.

You realize you are completely free of the concern that brought you here today, and that you no longer desire food that isn't good for you. You realize you have been given a second chance at complete health and happiness, and you are grateful to your body for the opportunity. You are pleased that you now only choose healthy foods to nourish your body.

As you continue to move along the path, you feel strong and free, healthy and happy, glad to be here, and glad to be you. As you continue along the path, you hear the seagulls, and the ocean waves, and you feel the sun warming your head and your shoulders, you feel the breeze against your skin, as you breathe deeply and freely, filling your lungs with life-giving oxygen. You enjoy a relaxing and refreshing walk whenever you get the opportunity. And as you continue to move along the path, you realize that we are coming closer to the pastoral area with the barn, and you look back one more time to see this beautiful place, and to remember evermore, how wonderful and alive you feel now that you are free of the challenge that brought you here originally. You look younger and feel younger every day. Your body thanks you for taking such good care of it.

As you continue to move along the path, your feet touch the gravel and as you look around, you notice the duck pond up ahead on the left and the red barn up ahead on the right. The cows are still grazing peacefully and the leaves rustle in the breeze. You see the large oak door up ahead and move forward toward it.

You arrive at the door and pull it open, the hinges squeaking again. You are now in the large round foyer with the stairs up ahead. You move toward the stairs and begin to move up them.

Number 1

Number 2

Number 3.......Coming back.

Number 4.......Coming back.

Number 5.......Coming back slowly.......coming back.

Number 6.......Coming back to the current moment and place.....coming back.

Number 7.......Coming back...feeling rested and refreshed....coming back.

Number 8.......Coming back...feeling good, feeling fine, perfectly relaxed.

Number 9...... Coming back now, eyes open, wide awake, eyes open, wide awake.

Number 10.....Eyes open, wide awake, eyes open wide awake.

WEIGHT LOSS SESSION SCRIPT 3

As you continue to move along the beach, you feel the sun warming the top of your head, and you feel the sea breeze against your skin, and you hear the sounds of children's laughter. To your right, you see the ocean, and the sun as it dances on the surface of the ocean. You can hear the sounds of sea gulls as they fly above the water, and as they dive into the water, happy to be alive, just like you, and as you continue to breathe deeply filling your lungs with life-giving oxygen.

You are amazed at the remarkable beauty of this place, and you feel great... happy, healthy, glad to be alive... glad to be here, and glad to be you. As you walk along the beach, you are thinking how much you enjoy having control over your body size and shape. It seems like an obvious thing, but for awhile you didn't. And now, being able to wear whatever you want to wear and looking good in it, and knowing that this will be true for the rest of your life......it's a truly wonderful feeling.

As you continue to walk along the beach, you enjoy feeling healthy and whole; you realize that this magical place has caused a complete transformation in you. You realize that you have left behind the concerns that brought you here today. It's so good to be able to eat what you enjoy and enjoy what you eat. No more guilty pleasures for you, just good, healthy food. You feel free, healthy, and strong, as you move along the beach. You breathe deeply, filling your lungs with life-giving oxygen, and as you move along the beach, you notice that your clothes are a little loose which really makes you happy. You allow yourself a moment to feel really proud of the changes you've made in your body and your thinking. And the irony is that given the choice, you would never go back to eating the way you used to eat. You have so much energy now and feel so energetic all the time. It's amazing.

As you continue to move along the beach, you notice a large group of people ahead on your right. These people are active, and happy, playing with a beach ball while others are playing volleyball. These people are active, trim, and happy, and as you observe these people, you pick up their general happiness which you attribute to their healthy diet and physical activity. You breathe deeply as you walk along, and as you do, you feel your youth returning, and your breath deepening, and you feel grateful to be here, and happy to be you. You marvel at your body's ability to easily and effortlessly change the habits of a lifetime so easily. You love your new life and you are grateful that your appetite is so easily satisfied with yummy, healthy food.

As you continue along the beach, you breathe deeply and easily. You feel your clothes growing looser on your body, as your metabolism adjusts favorably to the changes you are making. You feel your body strengthen, and as it does, your metabolism improves, in fact, your entire body responds favorably to these changes. You crave only healthy food these days.

You realize that it is time to return, so you turn around on the beach, heading back toward the path, waving at your new friends who are still playing and laughing and expressing all the health and well-being they enjoy. You feel grateful to be a part of that group of healthy and happy people. You enjoy following a healthy eating plan; in fact, you eat much more food than you used to eat because your metabolism works so well. It's great!

You realize you are completely free of the concerns that originally brought you here to the beach, and that you no longer want to do anything that doesn't completely support your physical health, wellbeing, and appearance. You realize you have been given a second chance at complete health and happiness, and you are grateful to your mind and body for the opportunity. You love your body, and you know that your body loves you too.

As you continue to move along the path, you feel strong and free, healthy and happy, glad to be here, and glad to be you. As you continue along the path, you hear the seagulls, and the ocean waves, and you feel the sun warming your head and your shoulders, you feel the breeze against your skin, as you breathe deeply and freely, filling your lungs with life-giving oxygen. You are enjoying this walk, feeling healthy and strong and really happy. You are proud of yourself and the way your body looks and feels. And as you continue to move along the path, you realize that we are coming closer to the pastoral area with the barn, and you look back one more time to see this beautiful place, and to remember evermore, how wonderful and alive you feel now that you are free of the challenge that brought you here. You decide in this moment, that you will never return to your old ways of eating. You are so happy just as you are.

As you continue to move along the path, your feet touch the gravel and as you look around, you notice the duck pond up ahead on the left and the red barn up ahead on the right. The cows are still grazing peacefully and the leaves rustle in the breeze. You see the large oak door up ahead and move forward toward it.

You arrive at the door and pull it open, the hinges squeaking again. You are now in the large round foyer with the stairs up ahead. You move toward the stairs and start to move up them.

Number 1

Number 2

Number 3.......Coming back.

Number 4.......Coming back.

Number 5.......Coming back slowly.......coming back.

Number 6.......Coming back to the current moment and place.....coming back.

Number 7.......Coming back...feeling rested and refreshed....coming back.

Number 8.......Coming back...feeling good, feeling fine, perfectly relaxed.

Number 9...... Coming back now, eyes open, wide awake, eyes open, wide awake.

Number 10.....Eyes open, wide awake, eyes open wide awake.

STRESS REDUCTION HYPNOSIS SERIES

Stress Reduction is another hypnosis application that does really well with a series of sessions. Generally, with Self Hypnosis, use the first session for about two weeks daily and then move onto the second session, and so on. For professional Hypnosis, use your own judgment as to how long to use each session script.

The word "seashell" has been embedded in the first script so that anyone who uses this script will recognize the use of the word "seashell" in the conscious state as a word that acts as an immediately calming influence. The use of the word "seashell" acts as a trigger or anchor to calm you or the client feels on the beach during sessions. This is a word to use in the event you feel yourself getting stressed or upset in the conscious state, as you go about your life. The use of this word will quickly help to alleviate any building tension or stress and the repetitious use of the word will strengthen its power.

If you are working professionally with clients, then explaining the way that the trigger word works while your client is in the conscious state is ideal.

With this series and the weight loss series, we have used similar script templates with different key suggestions for each script, so even though the script structure may seem very familiar to readers of Quantum Self Hypnosis and to NEIH graduates and students, these scripts are filled with new and unique suggestions.

STRESS REDUCTION SESSION 1

As you continue to move along the beach, you feel the sun warming the top of your head, you feel the sea breeze against your skin, and you hear the sounds of children's laughter as you move along the beach. To your right, you see the ocean and the sun as it dances on the surface of the water, you can hear the sounds of sea gulls as they fly above the water and as they dive into the water - happy to be alive just like you. As you continue to breathe deeply, filling your lungs with life-giving oxygen, you feel yourself growing calmer and calmer. The calm of the beach and the ocean soothes your soul. Any concerns or cares you brought here to the beach with you dissipate and disappear. You are amazed at the remarkable beauty of this place, and you feel great - happy, healthy, glad to be alive, glad to be here, and glad to be you. You breathe deeply and evenly, filling your lungs with calming and relaxing oxygen.

You feel any sense of tension in your body melt away, feeling free and young and full of life, certain of a happy outcome for this and every day. As you move along the beach you feel yourself relaxing, breathing deeply, feeling good, feeling fine with a light heart and a happy mind.

As you move along the beach, you see other people walking and talking along the beach, you see others lying on beach towels enjoying the beautiful day, and you feel a part of this happy scene. You are a good and happy person, who is consistently patient with others. You have a sense of belonging here, you feel accepted and valued by the others as well as by yourself. You realize that from this moment forward, you have a clearer view of whom you really are, and how well you fit into the world. You let out a deep sigh and with that sigh, you release any stored tension that might still be in your body. You feel so at peace and peaceful, that you realize you no longer have a desire to react to outside stimuli that used to bother you. You choose to be free of any upsets and to maintain your present sense of peace and calm.

You acknowledge that you are free of any concerns you might have carried around with you before today. You feel as if someone has given you a crystal ball that allows you to see all of the outcomes ahead for you, and you see that all is well. You are calm and at peace. You are a good and happy person. You take a deep breath and as you do, you feel your body bathing in the extra oxygen you are providing to it with your full and deep breathing. You decide to be patient with others at work, at home and in the world. You feel your heart open with happiness at this freeing decision, as you leave any concerns or worries behind.

As you continue to breathe deeply, you feel yourself becoming more and more relaxed moment by moment. You realize that this level of relaxation is now yours, without any effort on your part. You are looking forward to sharing this peace with others as you decide to be consistently kind and patient with others, and to no longer let petty annoyances rattle you.

As you continue to move along the beach, you see a beautiful seashell lying there in front of you. As you pick it up to admire it, you realize that this seashell can be your reminder of this perfect sense of relaxation you are enjoying today. From this moment forward, the word "seashell" causes your body to return to this perfect sense of relaxation. And as you look at the seashell, you feel a deeper sense of relaxation moving over you. Then you say the word "seashell" and you feel an even deeper sense of relaxation move over your body. And with this, you feel a true and abiding sense of the perfection of your world, and your place in the world. You realize that you are free forever more of any concerns or worries that might have occupied your mind before this day. You enjoy taking another deep breath, and as you do, your body relaxes even more.

As you continue to move along the beach, you see so many seashells on the beach, and just for fun, you say seashell, seashell, seashell, and each time that you do, you feel your body respond positively by relaxing more and more to the word that has become a signal for your body to relax.

And as you move along the beach, you breathe deeply and you realize how healing it is to breathe deeply. You feel your body respond to all of the oxygen that you are taking in. You decide that from this moment forward, you breathe deeply and fully, filling your body with life-giving oxygen.

As you continue to walk along the beach, you smell the saltwater and you hear the seagulls as they swoop and dive, happy to be alive and you feel happy too, and glad to be alive, just like the seagulls. You feel the sun warming your face and your shoulders, you feel the salt-breeze as it caresses you skin, you see the sun as it sparkles on the ocean, and you breathe deeply and freely, enjoying the day and enjoying being you. You are a good and happy person, newly determined to be patient with yourself and others, and looking forward to a more peaceful existence.

As you continue along the path, you hear the seagulls and the ocean waves, you feel the sun warming your head and your shoulders, and you feel the breeze against your skin as you breathe deeply and freely, filling your lungs with life-giving oxygen.

As you continue to move along the path, you realize that we are coming closer to the pastoral area with the barn. You look back one more time to see this beautiful beach and to remember evermore how wonderful and alive you feel now that you are free of the challenge that brought you here today; and how grateful you feel for this experience.

As you continue to move along the path, your feet touch the gravel and as you look around, you notice the duck pond up ahead on the left and the red barn up ahead on the right. The cows are still grazing peacefully and the leaves rustle in the breeze. You see the large oak door up ahead and move forward toward it.

You arrive at the door and pull it open, the hinges squeaking again. You are now in the large round foyer with the stairs up ahead. You move toward the stairs and begin to move up them.

Number 1

Number 2

Number 3.......Coming back.

Number 4.......Coming back.

Number 5.......Coming back slowly.......coming back.

Number 6.......Coming back to the current moment and place.....coming back.

Number 7.......Coming back...feeling rested and refreshed....coming back.

Number 8.......Coming back...feeling good, feeling fine, perfectly relaxed.

Number 9...... Coming back now, eyes open, wide awake, eyes open, wide awake.

Number 10.....Eyes open, wide awake, eyes open wide awake.

STRESS REDUCTION SESSION 2

As you continue to move along the beach, you feel the sun warming the top of your head, and you feel the sea breeze against your skin, and you hear the sounds of children's laughter. To your right, you see the ocean, and the sun as it dances on the surface of the ocean.

You can hear the sounds of sea gulls as they fly above the water, and as they dive into the water, happy to be alive, just like you, and as you continue to breathe deeply filling your lungs with life-giving oxygen, the colors of the children's swimsuits catch your eye... bright reds, and lemon yellows, and sky blues. You are amazed at the remarkable beauty of this place, and you feel great... happy, healthy, glad to be alive... glad to be here, and glad to be you. You are happy with your life, and you are experiencing an increased appreciation for all your blessings.

As you continue to walk along the beach, you enjoy feeling healthy and whole; you realize that this magical place has caused a complete transformation for you. You realize that you have left behind the concerns and cares that brought you here originally. You find that you are becoming more patient with yourself and more patient with others. You feel free, and healthy, and strong, as you move along the beach. You breathe deeply, filling your lungs with life-giving oxygen, and as you move along the beach, you realize that you are a happier person day by day, and you feel very grateful for that.

As you continue to move along the beach, you notice a large group of people ahead on your right. These people are active, and happy, playing with a beach ball while others are playing volleyball. These people are active, trim, and happy, and as you observe these people, you feel their sense of calm and peace. That peace seems to emanate from them; their calm feels entirely contagious which is good. You enjoy being with others and you laugh easily these days. You breathe deeply as you walk along, and as you do, you feel your youth returning, and your breath deepening, and you feel grateful to be here, and happy to be you. You marvel at your body's ability to easily and effortlessly leave behind the concerns that brought you here originally. You are becoming a very patient and understanding person. You seem to have lost any inclination for knee jerk reactions. You are really happy with your progress, and happy with your life.

As you continue along the beach, you breathe deeply and easily. You feel your clothes growing looser on your body, as your metabolism adjusts favorably to the changes you are making. You feel your body strengthen, and as it does, your metabolism improves, in fact, your entire body responds favorably to these changes. You are happy with your life and your outlook.

You realize that it is time to return back the way you came, so you turn around on the beach, heading back toward the path, and you wave at your new friends, still playing and laughing and expressing all the health and well-being they enjoy. You feel grateful to be a part of that group of happy, relaxed and patient people. You are a happy person.

You realize you are completely free of the concerns that brought you here, and that you no longer choose to be reactive. You realize you have been given a second chance at complete health and happiness, and you are grateful to your mind and body for the opportunity. When you feel yourself starting to return to your old ways, you breathe deeply and a sense of calm returns to you.

As you continue to move along the path, you feel strong and free, healthy and happy, glad to be here, and glad to be you. As you continue along the path, you hear the seagulls, and the ocean waves; you feel the sun warming your head and your shoulders, and you feel the breeze against your skin, as you breathe deeply and freely, filling your lungs with life-giving oxygen. You are happy to be here and happy to be alive. And as you continue to move along the path, you realize that we are coming closer to the pastoral area with the barn, and you look back one more time to see this beautiful place, and to remember evermore, how wonderful and alive you feel now that you are free of the challenge that brought you here originally. You breathe deeply and easily, and then you count your blessings.

As you continue to move along the path, your feet touch the gravel and as you look around, you notice the duck pond up ahead on the left and the red barn up ahead on the right. The cows are still grazing peacefully and the leaves rustle in the breeze. You see the large oak door up ahead and move forward toward it.

You arrive at the door and pull it open, the hinges squeaking again. You are now in the large round foyer with the stairs up ahead. You move toward the stairs and begin to move up them.

Number 1

Number 2

Number 3.......Coming back.

Number 4.......Coming back.

Number 5.......Coming back slowly.......coming back.

Number 6.......Coming back to the current moment and place.....coming back.

Number 7.......Coming back...feeling rested and refreshed....coming back.

Number 8.......Coming back...feeling good, feeling fine, perfectly relaxed.

Number 9...... Coming back now, eyes open, wide awake, eyes open, wide awake.

Number 10.....Eyes open, wide awake, eyes open wide awake.

STRESS REDUCTION SESSION SCRIPT 3

As you continue to move along the beach, you feel the sun warming the top of your head, and you feel the sea breeze against your skin, and you hear the sounds of children's laughter. To your right, you see the ocean, and the sun as it dances on the surface of the ocean. You can hear the sounds of sea gulls as they fly above the water, and as they dive into the water, happy to be alive, just like you, and as you continue to breathe deeply filling your lungs with life-giving oxygen, you realize that you feel very proud of yourself. You are becoming a much more kind and patient person. You feel calm and in control almost all the time now.

You are amazed at the remarkable beauty of this place, and you feel great...happy, healthy, glad to be alive...glad to be here, and glad to be you.

As you continue to walk along the beach, you enjoy feeling healthy and whole; you realize that this magical place has caused a complete transformation for you. You realize that you have left behind the challenges that originally brought you to this beach. You are happy to realize that difficult situations don't unnerve you anymore. You feel calm and in control almost all the time now. You feel free, healthy, and strong, as you move along the beach.

You breathe deeply, filling your lungs with life-giving oxygen, and as you move along the beach, you notice that your clothes are a little looser, and you feel that you are releasing an extra few pounds in the process of leaving this challenge behind you. People enjoy being with you more and more all the time now, and that makes you happy. You like being the steady and patient guy that people can tell their troubles to.

As you continue to move along the beach, you notice a large group of people ahead on your right. These people are active, and happy, playing with a beach ball while others are playing volleyball. These people are active, trim, and happy, and as you observe these people, you get a strong sense of their calm under all that play and laughter. You breathe deeply as you walk along, and as you do, you feel your youth returning, and your breath deepening, and you feel grateful to be here, and happy to be you. You marvel at your body's ability to easily and effortlessly leave behind the concern that brought you here originally. You are now one of the most relaxed people you know.

As you continue along the beach, you breathe deeply and easily. You feel your clothes growing looser on your body, as your metabolism adjusts favorably to the changes you are making. You feel your body strengthen, and as it does, your metabolism improves, in fact, your entire body responds favorably to these changes. You are happy to be living your life in a way that supports your continuing health.

You realize that it is almost time to return, and you turn around on the beach, heading back toward the path; and you wave at your new friends, still playing and laughing and expressing all the health and well-being they enjoy.

You feel grateful to be a part of that group of healthy and happy people. People enjoy being with you more and more all the time. You are the friendly guy with a smile for everyone.

You realize you are almost completely free of the challenges that brought you here originally, and that you no longer desire to do anything that isn't based in peace. You realize you have been given a second chance at complete health and happiness, and you are grateful to your body for the opportunity. Since you know that you control your own response to all situations that arise, you feel healthier and happier all the time. No more dramatic mood swings or stony looks cast at others. You enjoy being easy going and friendly.

As you continue to move along the path, you feel strong and free, healthy and happy, glad to be here, and glad to be you. As you continue along the path, you hear the seagulls, and the ocean waves, and you feel the sun warming your head and your shoulders; you feel the breeze against your skin, as you breathe deeply and freely, filling your lungs with life-giving oxygen. As you continue to breathe deeply, your body releases any tiny tensions that may exist within you. And as you continue to move along the path, you realize that we are coming closer to the pastoral area with the barn, and you look back one more time to see this beautiful place, and to remember evermore, how wonderful and alive you feel now that you are freer of the challenge that brought you here. You are one of the most relaxed people you know and you are so grateful to be that person. You are a happy person now, and you are proud of yourself.

As you continue to move along the path, your feet touch the gravel and as you look around, you notice the duck pond up ahead on the left and the red barn up ahead on the right. The cows are still grazing peacefully and the leaves rustle in the breeze. You see the large oak door up ahead and move forward toward it.

You arrive at the door and pull it open, the hinges squeaking again. You are now in the large round foyer with the stairs up ahead. You move toward the stairs and begin to move up them.

Number 1

Number 2

Number 3.......Coming back.

Number 4.......Coming back.

Number 5.......Coming back slowly.......coming back.

Number 6.......Coming back to the current moment and place.....coming back.

Number 7.......Coming back...feeling rested and refreshed....coming back.

Number 8.......Coming back...feeling good, feeling fine, perfectly relaxed.

Number 9...... Coming back now, eyes open, wide awake, eyes open, wide awake.

Number 10.....Eyes open, wide awake, eyes open wide awake.

CHAPTER 4

MASTER HYPNOSIS INDUCTIONS

These Master Hypnosis Inductions are the core tools for creating Hypnosis sessions, taking yourself or a client from the waking state to a medium state of hypnosis. Adding one of these Master Inductions on the front end of a Hypnosis script creates a full hypnosis session. We have included these inductions for those who aren't currently working with Hypnosis and thus need an induction to create a complete Hypnosis session script, and for those who are always on the lookout for a new Master Hypnosis Induction.

We have included a Classic Master Hypnosis Induction as well as one of our newer Quick Inductions.

CLASSIC MASTER HYPNOSIS INDUCTION

This is a longer induction and takes about 30 minutes to transition from the waking state to a full medium state of Hypnosis. It features a "big relax" at the beginning, then the classic Count-down, the Path,[Insert Hypnosis session script here]. The dots and commas are here to indicate extended pauses, helping you to cadence more easily.

[Begin Induction]

As you continue to breathe deeply, I would like you to allow your body to become more and more relaxed. And as your body becomes more and more relaxed, you can feel a tingling on the top of your head. Feel the top of your head becoming more and more relaxed. As you continue to become more and more relaxed, perfectly at peace, perfectly at ease, perfectly safe, and perfectly secure, your relaxation deepens.

And as you continue to become more and more relaxed, you feel that wonderful sense of relaxation traveling down the back of your head; you may have a sense of warmth and a sense of tingling as you become more and more relaxed, more and more at peace, welcoming this gentle and warm relaxation that is filling your body.

As you continue to become more and more relaxed, you can feel this sense of relaxation moving down the front of your face, as you feel the tiny muscles around your eyes relaxing, and the corners of your mouth relaxing, and your jaw relaxing. Throughout this process, you feel your eyelids becoming heavier and heavier as you become more perfectly relaxed and more perfectly at peace.

As you become more and more relaxed, you feel yourself breathing more deeply, you feel yourself taking deep relaxing breaths of air, as you fill your lungs with oxygen and your body, with a deepening sense of relaxation.

As you continue to become more and more relaxed, you feel this wonderful sense of calm and peace moving down your neck relaxing your shoulders and down your chest. As you feel yourself becoming more and more relaxed, you find it is so easy to breathe deeply, filling your lungs with life-giving oxygen as you become more and more relaxed.

As you become more and more relaxed, you feel this relaxation moving down the front of your body, relaxing your hips and your knees as it moves down your body, all the way to your feet. As you continue to breathe deeply, you can feel the bottoms of your feet tingling and becoming perfectly relaxed.

As you become more and more perfectly relaxed, you feel the relaxation moving down your back and down the backs of your legs until all of you is completely relaxed.

As you continue to breathe deeply, becoming more and more relaxed, perfectly at ease, perfectly at peace, you feel yourself moving forward toward a wide set of well-lit stairs. They remind you of a large beautiful set of stone steps you saw in an art museum at some point in time, and you feel yourself looking forward to walking down these stairs. You feel safe as you think about moving down these well-lighted stairs.

As you find yourself moving toward these stairs, you have a sense of anticipation. You are looking forward to moving down these stairs, and you feel perfectly safe, perfectly secure, as you continue forward.

As you move down the steps, I will count backwards from 10-1. When you reach one, you will be perfectly relaxed, in your own natural state of relaxation. Counting down now....

[You will repeat the phrases shown below for each step, 2-3 times slowly, which will allow you to spend about 3 minutes at each step.]

~Number 10 - Feeling good, feeling fine, perfectly safe, perfectly secure; as you continue to breathe deeply, you feel yourself surrendering to the deep and perfect relaxation that is filling your body. And you feel fine, perfectly safe, perfectly secure...moving down...going deeper and deeper...

Number 9 - As you continue to move down the stairs, you feel yourself becoming more and more relaxed, perfectly at peace, feeling good, feeling fine, perfectly safe, perfectly secure and as you continue to breathe deeply, you feel yourself surrendering to the deep and perfect relaxation that is filling your body. And you feel fine, perfectly safe, perfectly secure...moving down...going deeper and deeper...

Number 8 - As you continue to move down the stairs, you feel yourself becoming more and more relaxed, perfectly at peace, feeling good, feeling fine, perfectly safe, perfectly secure and as you continue to breathe deeply, you feel yourself surrendering to the deep and perfect relaxation that is filling your body. And you feel fine, perfectly safe, perfectly secure...moving down...going deeper and deeper. Every sound that you hear only causes you to go deeper and deeper, deeper and deeper, deeper and deeper.

Number 7 - Feeling good, feeling fine, perfectly safe, perfectly secure, as you continue to breathe deeply, you feel yourself surrendering to the deep and perfect relaxation that is filling your body. And you feel fine, perfectly safe, perfectly secure...moving down...going deeper and deeper... Every number you hear causes you to go deeper and deeper. As you continue to move down the stairs, you feel yourself becoming more and more relaxed, perfectly at peace, feeling good, feeling fine, perfectly safe, and perfectly secure. As you continue to breathe deeply, you feel yourself surrendering to the deep and perfect relaxation that is filling your body. And you feel fine, perfectly safe, perfectly secure...moving down...going deeper and deeper. Every sound that you hear causes you to go deeper and deeper, deeper and deeper, deeper and deeper.

Number 6 - As you continue to move down the stairs, you feel yourself becoming more and more relaxed, perfectly at peace, feeling good, feeling fine, perfectly safe, perfectly secure and as you continue to breathe deeply, you feel yourself surrendering to the deep and perfect relaxation that is filling your body. And you feel fine, perfectly safe, perfectly secure...moving down...going deeper and deeper...

Number 5 - Feeling good, feeling fine, perfectly safe, perfectly secure, as you continue to breathe deeply, you feel yourself surrendering to the deep and perfect relaxation that is filling your body. And you feel fine, perfectly safe, perfectly secure...moving down...going deeper and deeper... Every number you hear causes you to go deeper and deeper. As you continue to move down the stairs, you feel yourself becoming more and more relaxed, perfectly at peace, feeling good, feeling fine, perfectly safe, and perfectly secure. As you continue to breathe deeply, you feel yourself surrendering to the deep and perfect relaxation that is filling your body. And you feel fine, perfectly safe, perfectly secure...moving down...going deeper and deeper. Every sound that you hear causes you to go deeper and deeper, deeper and deeper, deeper and deeper.

Number 4 - Feeling good, feeling fine, perfectly safe, perfectly secure, as you continue to breathe deeply, you feel yourself surrendering to the deep and perfect relaxation that is filling your body. And you feel fine, perfectly safe, perfectly secure...moving down...going deeper and deeper... Every number you hear causes you to go deeper and deeper. As you continue to move down the stairs, you feel yourself becoming more and more relaxed, perfectly at peace, feeling good, feeling fine, perfectly safe, and perfectly secure. As you continue to breathe deeply, you feel yourself surrendering to the deep and perfect relaxation that is filling your body. And you feel fine, perfectly safe, perfectly secure...moving down...going deeper and deeper. Every sound that you hear causes you to go deeper and deeper, deeper and deeper, deeper and deeper.

Number 3 -Feeling good, feeling fine, perfectly safe, perfectly secure, as you continue to breathe deeply, you feel yourself surrendering to the deep and perfect relaxation that is filling your body. And you feel fine, perfectly safe, perfectly secure...moving down...going deeper and deeper... Every number you hear causes you to go deeper and deeper. As you continue to move down the stairs, you feel yourself becoming more and more relaxed, perfectly at peace, feeling good, feeling fine, perfectly safe, and perfectly secure. As you continue to breathe deeply, you feel yourself surrendering to the deep and perfect relaxation that is filling your body. And you feel fine, perfectly safe, perfectly secure...moving down...going deeper and deeper. Every sound that you hear causes you to go deeper and deeper, deeper and deeper, deeper and deeper.

Number 2 - Feeling good, feeling fine, perfectly safe, perfectly secure, as you continue to breathe deeply, you feel yourself surrendering to the deep and perfect relaxation that is filling your body. And you feel fine, perfectly safe, perfectly secure...moving down...going deeper and deeper... Every number you hear causes you to go deeper and deeper. As you continue to move down the stairs, you feel yourself becoming more and more relaxed, perfectly at peace, feeling good, feeling fine, perfectly safe, and perfectly secure. As you continue to breathe deeply, you feel yourself surrendering to the deep and perfect relaxation that is filling your body. And you feel fine, perfectly safe, perfectly secure...moving down...going deeper and deeper. Every sound that you hear causes you to go deeper and deeper, deeper and deeper, deeper and deeper.

Number 1 - As you continue to breathe deeply, you feel yourself becoming more and more relaxed, perfectly at peace, perfectly at ease, perfectly safe, perfectly secure, happy and feeling fine. You are now at the perfect state of relaxation.

[Transition into the Path Script, if you choose to use it. The Path script introduces NLP prompts to heighten the reality experience for the client or you.]

PATH SCRIPT COMPONENT

[Begin Script]

And as you reach the bottom of the stairs, you find yourself in a large round room with floor to ceiling windows, and you see the sunlight streaming thru the windows, warming the flagstone floor.

And up ahead you see a large oak door; you feel drawn to the door and have a sense of anticipation at the thought of moving through this doorway.

You move forward and grasp the brass door handle, and pull the door open, and as you do, you hear the hinges squeak as you move thru the doorway into a beautiful pastoral area.

And as you look around, you see on your left a large, red barn with a shiny metal roof. You see the sun glancing off the roof, and you are amazed at how bright the red of the barn is. As you continue to look, you see 2 black and white cows grazing contentedly in the pasture in front of the barn. As you watch them, you have a sense of their peace and contentment, and you find yourself taking on some of that peace and contentment as you walk along the path.

As you move along the path, you hear the sound of the gravel crunching under your feet and you feel the cool breeze against your skin... you hear the birds in the trees above your head, you smell the flowers growing alongside the gravel path... you hear the sound of the breeze as it moves through the trees... you feel the roughness of the gravel on the path through your shoes, and you hear the sounds the cows are making as they eat the grass growing in the pasture.

As you continue to move along the path, you see a duck pond up ahead on the right, and as you look you can see 2 ducks playing in the pond, you hear the sounds they make as they play in the water, and you can see how much fun they are having as they play in the water... you hear the sounds as they play and as you continue to watch them, you notice to the left of the pond a field of daisies, and you see how the white and yellow of their flowers contrast with the green of the grass, and you see how beautiful and magical this place is.

As you continue to move along the path, you hear the sound of the birds in the trees, and you feel the breeze against your skin, and you feel the sun warming your head and your shoulders as you move along the path.

And as you move along the path, you feel the crunch of the gravel under your feet, and you hear the sounds of the birds in the trees and you feel the breeze against your skin, and you have a sense of the beauty of this magical place.

As you continue to move along the path, you notice that the path is changing to sand and as you continue to look around you notice that you are in a beautiful beach area.

[Transition into the Behavior Modification Script Component]

RIVER QUICK MASTER HYPNOSIS INDUCTION

Read this script very slowly with exaggerated pauses every 3 or 6 words. For Self Hypnosis, always start with your eyes closed in a comfortable chair at a quiet time. Cell phones off. The dots in this script indicate the suggested pauses.

[Begin Script]

As you sit back and breathe deeply... you remember a time... when you were younger... a child really... without a care and on that day... you were floating peacefully... in the water... weightless... drifting... easy... contented... carried along gently... by the water... drifting away... drifting away... peaceful... weightless... free as a bird. You may have been in a swimming pool... it may have been a lake... it may have been a river... it doesn't matter... you remember the lovely times you had there... playing in the water... floating in the water...

Imagine a perfect day and on this day... imagine that you were floating... on an inflatable raft down a gentle... meandering river... feeling the buoyancy... of the water... gently lifting you... carrying you... supporting you... as you drift away... floating weightless... in the water... loving that feeling of peace... contented... effortless pleasure... feeling your muscles relax completely... feeling your breathing change... slowing... slowing... deeper and deeper... allowing yourself to drift in and out... of a perfect... dream-like state... floating... safe... secure... protected... down and down... the river you float... you drift... easy and gentle... happy and peaceful. As you listen... to my voice... your mind relaxes... easily and peacefully. Effortlessly... deeper and deeper... deeper and deeper, you drift into a lovely sleep-like state.

As you continue... to drift... on that slow... and gentle river... if you allow yourself... you can hear the water lapping gently... moving downward toward the lake... you enjoy the feeling... of the sun... peeking through the canopy... of leaves overhead... protecting you... from the heat of the day. The sun gently... caresses your skin... and you hear... the sounds of birds chirping... the leaves rustling... in the gentle breeze... as you drift away going deeper... and deeper... into that easy... peaceful place... your mind at peace... cares all washed away... gently rocking in the peaceful water... as you allow yourself... to go deeper... and deeper... into that dream-like state... of perfect contentment... perfectly safe... perfectly at ease... Nurtured... protected and secure... feeling free of any concerns.

As you continue to breathe gently... you feel yourself slipping away into a peaceful, happy place... calm... protected... secure... peaceful... quiet... deeper and deeper... a perfect place... your muscles are so relaxed... you can barely feel your arms or legs. They're weightless... you love this feeling... floating... easy... gentle. You're less aware of the water now... and your awareness of my voice increases… my words reminds you of this perfect world… you feel safe… protected… happy … relaxed... calm and you know… that these feelings... will remain with you… for a long time. This calm… will never fade away.

Everything in your outer awareness… everything but this beautiful place… and this beautiful calm fades… as you become so relaxed… so peaceful that my voice gets softer… and softer… and softer as you enter… the perfect state… of relaxation. You can still hear… my voice… as I guide you along through this beautiful place… the sound of my voice is in the background now… as you focus on the sights, sounds, and lovely scents all around you. Your full awareness… is focused… on this moment and the sights and sounds of this beautiful place.

As you continue to float… going deeper and deeper, deeper and deeper… into that calm… you feel your body… reach the perfect state… of relaxation… you sigh… with pleasure… at the total calm… and peace you feel.

Perfectly safe… perfectly at ease… perfectly secure…
perfectly protected.

[End Script]

Transition into your Hypnosis Session Script.

CHAPTER 5

SUCCESS GUIDELINES

This chapter is a condensed and edited version of a similar chapter found in *Quantum Self Hypnosis* and addresses the effect that the changes you make, after using Self Hypnosis, has on family and friends.

What's good for you isn't always perceived by those around you as good for them. As a group, humans don't like change. Some of us don't even like surprises because surprise usually involves change, right? That's got to be wrong thinking, though, because personal growth is change and that's always a good thing. Isn't it? Yes and no.

Working hard to create personal growth represents a real personal victory. But be prepared for some resistance from those around you because.....humans generally don't like change, particularly change they didn't initiate.

The new you that you worked so hard to manifest may feel a bit foreign to you, but to others it likely feels as if the person they've known is gone and a stranger is in your place.

Throughout the years that you were "old" you, you had numerous interactions with family and close friends, as well as more casual contacts. In the course of those years, you taught people who you are. They learned what to expect from you, how much you would put up with, and how to get their way with you. We all teach those around us how to manage us. In fact, we teach them well.

Individuals who feel less than they really are often put up with a lot more than they should, in terms of behavior they accept from other people. Those around us learn what to expect from us, but when we change and become thinner, more confident, more relaxed, and more powerful, the way we interact with others changes. We expect more and frequently put up with less than we used to. As you might imagine, the "new" you is often a big surprise to those around you. You're different, more confident, and less easy to manage. Yes, you look better and are happier and more fun, but interacting with you can be a lot more work than it used to be.

This adjustment period with friends, family and acquaintances can be managed more easily if you expect it and prepare for it. People are funny. They can want you to be thinner or more relaxed and yet when you accomplish these goals, they can feel threatened. I think of it this way. When you've known someone for a long time, he or she has "learned" you; in some ways you're like part of the wallpaper. You're a constant and thus require a lot less attention than you did at the beginning of your interaction.

When you change your mind and/or your body, it will probably require some work for others to re-learn you. As mentioned earlier, most people don't like it when anything changes, so when a person in their sphere changes all the rules because he/she has experienced a huge personal growth spurt, the transition isn't always seamless.

213

Can you stop others from reacting to the changes in you? No. Many will celebrate your great success, a few will resent it and a few will find it very inconvenient. This is natural and it will pass. Be who you are, celebrate your own success, be kind and patient as others adjust to the new you, but don't give up any ground. Achieving personal growth always comes at a price. To transition from "old" you to "new" you required a lot of effort and commitment on your part. You've made it and achieved what many never will. It is cause for celebration and if everyone isn't celebrating right away, trust that they will when they get used to the new you. Some relationships may not make the transition, but that's okay. There's an expression that has always given me a lot of comfort as I've transitioned through my own growth stages. No one can take away what's truly yours, and conversely you can't hold onto what's not. Relationships that fail to make the transition would have failed at some point anyway. And honestly, if you're in a relationship with someone who values his/her own convenience above your happiness; is that a relationship you want to continue?

This is all the good news. You've set goals for yourself and accomplished them which is the bottom line. And forewarned is forearmed. Expect the best of everyone, but don't come unglued if everyone doesn't embrace the new you right off the bat. Those people in your life who are keepers will ride the wave of your personal growth cycles and celebrate your successes with you, as they stay by your side learning this new and improved version of you!

CHAPTER 6

SUMMARY

You have many tools available to you in this book, to create a better life for yourself, clients and friends. It's my hope that you've already discovered the magic of Hypnosis and that you are adding to your library of Hypnosis scripts, or that you are on your first journey into improving your life with Self Hypnosis, or you are a working professional in the field of Hypnosis, busy helping others. In any of those cases, I sincerely hope that you have found value in reading this book.

If you're a Hypnosis or Hypnotherapy professional, then you are all set; you know exactly how to use these scripts to help others. If you are going to be using this book in your Self Hypnosis journey, then I have a few suggestions for you that will help you to succeed. If you are a working professional, please consider sharing some of these thoughts with your clients, in an effort to prepare them for the transition to a better and happier life.

Be patient. I still believe that patience is one of the keys to achieving your highest outcome. Be kind to yourself and be patient with yourself. Take one day at a time and give yourself the gift of your undivided attention for 45 minutes daily while you enjoy your Self Hypnosis session. Make that session a priority and organize around it whenever possible. If you are working with a Certified Hypnotherapist, then commit to the program this professional has designed for you.

Be kind. As you change, the people in your life will need to change too, to accommodate the changes in you. Be kind to them and to yourself. Change is almost always good because change promotes growth, but change isn't always easy. Kindness can ease the way for everyone who is in your circle of influence.

Be positive. Once you start on a Hypnosis program for yourself or someone else, assume that it's already a done deal. Assume that the changes have already occurred and that you're just waiting for those changes to show up in present reality.

Don't second guess yourself. Trust this process. As you use Self Hypnosis, you will find that you feel happier, more rested, sleep better and just feel better overall. Trust that you're on the right path and continue to move forward on that path.

Enjoy the process. You may not realize this, but you are engaging in a magical process. Let's face it. You relax deeply, listen to 8 or 9 suggestions while you are in a relaxed state and your life improves. If it's not magical, I don't know what is.

Keep a journal. I know journaling is in style, but that's not why I'm suggesting it. If you were going to see a professional Certified Hypnotherapist, he would be keeping a file of your sessions and the progress you're making. As the client or Self-Hypnotist, it's valuable for you to keep some notes on the changes you're making. You're important and so is this process. Keeping track of your thoughts and the changes you make in your life will have a lot of value for you as you look back, after creating your desired changes. It will make you happy to have a record of your experiences and your thoughts about the process while the process was occurring. Once you've achieved your goals, you can't go back and recapture this fleeting information. Taking an extra 5 minutes to note changes and thoughts every couple of days during this process will reward you grandly.

Look ahead. This is directed to the person using this book for Self Hypnosis. If you are like many users of Self Hypnosis, you may fall in love with the process and want to work in this field. Your practice with Self Hypnosis will stand you in good stead as you will develop confidence in the process. If you decide that you want to train as a Certified Clinical Hypnotherapist, please consider NEIH as your training source. As a reader of Hypnosis Scripts and a member of the *Hypnosis Scripts* member website, you will be eligible for a training discount. Please feel free to visit the NEIH website at http://neih.com/ for information on our training programs.

Join the Hypnosis Scripts website. First of all, it's free and joining will give you the FREE audio Weight Loss Hypnosis session valued at $59. The session will be helpful to readers who are planning to record their own sessions; the session demonstrates ideal timing, cadence and the general construction of the session. You can find the members' website at http://quantumhypnosisscripts.com. You will be able to access your Free Audio Hypnosis session on this page.

And last but not least, thank you for reading this book. Writing it was a labor of love and a source of real pleasure for me. Sharing this wonderful self-help modality with readers from around the globe is an honor and a privilege that I do not take lightly. I wish you every success in life and I hope you create the life of your dreams.

Lightning Source UK Ltd.
Milton Keynes UK
UKOW06f2015110515

251299UK00015B/532/P